RIDING the HOLLYWOOD TRAIL

Tales of the Silver Screen Cowboys

RIDING the HOLLYWOOD TRAIL

Tales of the Silver Screen Cowboys

CHARLIE LeSUEUR

A division of
FIVE STAR PUBLICATIONS, INC.
Chandler, AZ

Linda F. Radke, President
Five Star Publications, Inc.
PO Box 6698
Chandler, AZ 85246-6698
480-940-8182

www.RidingtheHollywoodTrail.com

Library of Congress Cataloging-in-Publication Data

LeSueur, Charlie.
  Riding the Hollywood trail : tales of the silver screen cowboys / by Charlie LeSueur.

    p. : ill. ; cm.

    ISBN-13: 978-1-58985-104-7
    ISBN-10: 1-58985-104-8

1. Western films--United States--History and criticism. 2. Motion picture actors and actresses--United States--Biography. I. Title.

PN1995.9.W4 L47 2008
791.43/6278

Printed in the United States of America

Cover Design: Kris Taft Miller

This book is dedicated to Uncle Ichi,
who read my first book and asked,
"Where's Hoot, Buck, Ken, Tim, and Battlin' Bob?"

Well, here they are!

TABLE OF CONTENTS

ACKNOWLEDGMENTS

I would like to thank the following people for their support:

Hank and Sharyn Sheffer, who've helped in making this book and my dreams come true.

Mary Brown, from the Festival of the West, for her belief in me all these years.

Mary Ellen Kay, for her friendship and support. For me her star will always shine bright.

My wife Dawn, for pestering me to get this book finished.

Johnny Western and Buck Taylor for giving me the idea for my first book, "The Legends Live On."

Cheryl Rogers-Barnett and Larry Barnett for their insight into the lives of Cheryl's mother and father, Roy and Dale, and the inner workings of Republic Studios.

To my father who gave me a love for these great films and the stars, and my mother for simply being my mom, and putting up with me for all these years – you're the best!

To my kids for learning all about the western stars, and even sitting through a few of their movies with me.

And to all the people who kept asking me when they could get their hands on this book. You can have it now!

—Charlie LeSueur
December 2001

INTRODUCTION

This book started out, many moons ago, as a salute to the western film heroes and their sidekicks.

The book, which was to be titled, *Fuzzy Who? Those Dynamic Western Duos of the Silver Screen* was frustrating due to the amount of information I had, and the many differing opinions of those involved in the stories. I would feel like my research was almost complete and then another piece of information would pop up that might dispute something I had written.

Having read so many books and articles that had errors, I didn't want that to happen to my second book. I don't believe that any work of non-fiction is ever completely error free, but the author would like to think that they have taken every step possible to make sure their information is faultless.

Another bane of the non-fiction writer is opinion. Everyone has an opinion, but I tried to walk a fine line and present facts to back up my opinions. As in the case of the relationship between Gene Autry and Smiley Burnette, my opinions are based on the facts I lay before you. I can, however, be quite out-spoken and the intended book would have been well over three hundred pages, and would have been completed sometime in the next fifty years to satisfy my desire for authenticity. As it is, this book took three years too long to finish when it should have only taken a year or less.

After several frustrating and sleepless nights I finally decided to forget the hero and sidekick theme, strip away the fat, and simply talk about the things that interest me— the roots of the B western film and the people who made these films possible. Most of what you'll find in these pages is culled from the intended book, just shortened and less ambitious in scope.

Now you may ask me, "Hey, Charlie, what's the difference in the book you intended to write and the one I'm reading now?" Well, the answer is easy—*About two hundred pages.*

Publicity photo of Mary Ellen Kay, dedicated to my daughter, Taylor.

FOREWARD
By Mary Ellen Kay

As long as I can remember I have been a zealous fan of western movies. I was first introduced to western films by, of all people, my mother. I'll never forget the time she took me to see my first film, *The Plainsman*, with Gary Cooper and Jean Arthur. The year was 1936. I was thrilled to think my mother was taking her seven-year-old daughter to the movies, and in the evening, which was unthinkable back then!

I discovered the movies were wonderful, true, and magical. From that point forward, I began attending Saturday matinees regularly at the Wellman Theater in Girard, Ohio, not far from my home in McDonald, Ohio.

I adored many of the actors on the screen, especially Hopalong Cassidy (Bill Boyd) who looked like an angel cowboy to me. Other actors who had a big influence on me were Tom Mix, Bob Steele, Ken Maynard, Buster Crabbe, Noah Beery, Jr., Allan "Rocky" Lane, Lash LaRue, "Wild Bill" Elliott, Charles Starrett, Johnny Mack Brown, and on and on the list goes.

This all built a foundation in my life. I knew I could ride horseback long before I ever did, but the Westerns made me believe I could. I learned by watching my heroes and heroines. I knew I could handle a gun; my father taught me when I was 13. We would target practice and I got to be a fairly good shot. The movies allowed me to dream and dream big. And, oh yes, my favorite song was "I Want to Be a Cowboy's Sweetheart." I never did get to kiss the cowboy—he would just ride out into the sunset and wave goodbye.

In August 1951, I signed a contract with Republic Studios after I completed, *Rodeo King and the Senorita*, with Rex Allen and Buddy Ebsen, with George Blair directing. He also directed *Silver City Bonanza* and *Thunder in God's Country*. William Whitney, a sweetheart of a man, directed me in the films I did with Rex and Slim Pickens – *Border Saddlemates, The Last Musketeer*, and *Colorado Sundown*. Singing with Rex in these films was a real thrill!!

In between, I made three movies with Allan "Rocky" Lane – *Wells Fargo Gunmaster, Fort Dodge Stampede*, and *Desert of Lost Men* – and a serial, sometimes working on two different films in one day. We made those Westerns in about 14 days and those were exciting times. I would get myself into the meat of the story and enjoyed being a part of it. Ironically, I did these films thinking they'd never be seen other than in their initial release.

In 1950 I did *Streets of Ghost Town* with Charlie Starrett for Columbia, and then *Vigilante Terror* in 1953 with "Wild Bill" Elliott, and *Yukon Vengeance* with Kirby Grant in 1954, for Allied Artists. I also had the distinct pleasure of working with Roy Rogers and Dale Evans on one of their TV shows.

Who would have thought that nearly 50 years later I would be attending Western film festivals across the country, sometimes the great seas, meeting folks I've worked with on films almost five decades ago, and witnessing how loyal Western film fans have been, and are today. They have faithfully kept the history and, more importantly, the values of the Western film heroes and heroines alive. They give of themselves so willingly in both their time and energy promoting these great film festivals everywhere, so that generation after generation will never forget how it was during the days when good and evil were clearly defined, and honor and respect were virtues that were sought after.

I thank God for allowing us to continue enjoying the fruits of our hero's labors, and for keeping it alive and well for future generations.

I first met Charlie and Dawn LeSueur, and their talented family, during the Festival of the West at Rawhide in Scottsdale, Arizona (where I live). They are surely one of the most delightful families I have ever met. Charlie and Dawn are very active at the festival, and Charlie reminds me so much of Alex Gordon, whom I have known, and loved, for a very long time. Like Alex, Charlie is a walking movie and actor encyclopedia. I can call him anytime and he will fill me in with dates, places, vital statistics, previous film work, background information, and even their mother's maiden names on a need to know basis! They are both genuine, kind and caring. I am indeed a very fortunate person to have such friends.

Thank you, Charlie, for asking me to write this foreword and to share my heart with your readers regarding my love for the Western motion picture.

Mary Ellen Kay
Mary Ellen Kay

Mary Ellen Kay's first film with Rex Allen, "Rodeo King and the Senorita." This was Buddy Ebsen's fourth film as Rex's sidekick. He would make one more with him.

Sentimental reunion between Mary Ellen, and Rex Allen. Music legend, Snuff Garrett is pictured with them. Snuff is responsible for the song, "The Last of the Silver Screen Cowboys".

PROLOGUE

The kind words that my great friend Mary Ellen Kay wrote pays me a terrific compliment by the comparison with Alex Gordon. British born Gordon, and his brother Richard, moved to New York in 1947. During his youth Alex had been the President of the Gene Autry Fan Club in his native England and, as a result, was able to correspond with Western stars like Ray "Crash" Corrigan, Buck Jones, George O' Brien and Tom Keene.

Gordon, obviously a great fan of the "Golden Years" of film, moved to Hollywood in 1952. During the next few years he would produce many films using well-known stars of the 30s and 40s.

He would work with infamous film director Ed Wood, writing **Bride of the Monster** starring Bela Lugosi. But Gordon also produced a number of popular 50s theatrical horror films for American International Pictures. These films hold a special place in the hearts of horror genre fans everywhere. As a child, I remember sitting in front of the television set watching films like *Atomic Submarine*, *The Day The World Ended*, *Voodoo Woman* (starring Mary Ellen Kay), and *The She Creature*. We all have special memories from our childhood and these films are some of mine.

Gordon loved the Western stars and used many of them in his films of the 50s. It's great to see familiar faces like Raymond Hatton, Kermit Maynard, Jack Perrin, and Dick Foran in his movies.

Later, in the 60s, Gordon would show his love for the Western genre with films like *The Bounty Killer* and *Requiem for a Gunfighter*, casting veteran western stars like Rod Cameron, Bob Steele, Col. Tim McCoy, Buster Crabbe, Richard Arlen, Dan Duryea, Johnny Mack Brown, and Fuzzy Knight. A special treat is watching Broncho Billy Anderson, at the time 86 years old, in *The Bounty Killer*.

For years Gordon worked alongside Gene Autry, but sadly he passed away on June 24, 2003.

The thing I envy most about Alex Gordon is the relationship he had with so many stars of years gone by. You can keep your Tom Cruises, Brad Pitts, and Julia Roberts. Give me people like Bob Steele, Buster Crabbe, Jack Holt, Buck Jones, Bela Lugosi, Mae March, Jane Darwell, Tom Conway, and Chester Morris, to mention just a few. A mixed bunch, but imagine the stories they could tell.

People like Mary Ellen Kay, beautiful inside and out, have great stories to tell, and the legendary Alex Gordon was there as well, mingling with the stars, and producing movies that will stand the test of time. They weren't *The Ten Commandments* or *Ben Hur*, but boy were they entertaining!

With this book I hope to share some of the knowledge I've been able to obtain, especially through the conversations I've had with people who were there.

Alex Gordon's knowledge of the stars, and his experience in the film business, was vast. It's something I would have loved to tap into. I am flattered that Ellen would compare me to such a man...very flattered indeed.

—Charlie LeSueur
July 2003

Producer Alex Gordon on Western backlot with Cowboy icon Johnny Mack Brown.

Alex Gordon talking with film legends Bob Steele and Col. Tim McCoy while they were filming, "Requiem for a Gunfighter" in 1965.

G. M. "Broncho Billy" Anderson

CHAPTER ONE
A COUPLE OF FORGOTTEN STARS
—or —
OUR NEW HERO'S NAME IS VINCENT MARKOWSKI?

Broncho Billy most assuredly started it all. Then came William S. Hart and Tom Mix. Then Buck Jones, Col. Tim McCoy, Hoot Gibson, Ken Maynard, Fred Thomson, and Leo Maloney.

"Wait a minute," you say. "Who the heck are Fred Thomson and Leo Maloney?" To start with, Fred Thomson was a true western star. For a time, he entered the realm of the "Big Five," Mix, Jones, McCoy, Gibson, and Maynard. He actually entered pictures before McCoy. He was as popular as they were, and was the first western star to have his own production company, something that was unheard of in those days.

Though Thomson was one of the most revered western stars during the silent era, exact information about him is hard to come by. Depending on what source material you read, he was either born in January or February of 1890 in Pasadena, California.

Extremely athletic, Thomson was a star fullback at Occidental Academy High and, at six-teen, he entered Occidental College, where he continued to play football, and was elected student council president in his senior year. In 1910 and 1911 he captured first place in the National Track and Field competitions, and in 1913 he beat the world's record in track and field set by sports great Jim Thorpe.

Like his father, he entered Princeton Theological Seminary to become a Presbyterian minister while continuing in sports. After serving as a pastor in Washington, D.C. and Los Angeles, Thomson was assigned to Goldfield, Nevada. He had, by this time, married his college sweetheart, Gail Jepson, and his life in the ministry seemed to be assured.

In 1916, however, an event would shake Thomson's life and faith, and send him on the road towards moviestardom. Gail died of tuberculosis. Soon after, Thomson enlisted in the army were he was commissioned as a second Lieutenant and assigned to Battery F of the 143rd Field Artillery as a Chaplain.

If not for joining the army, Thomson would probably never have made it into film. While arranging for an appearance of the 143rd in her film, *Johanna Enlists*, Mary Pickford met the handsome Thomson, while he was recuperating from a football injury he had sustained. Impressed with his handsome features, Mary introduced him to her best friend, screenwriter Frances Marion. They fell in love and would eventually marry in 1919, but not before both of them where sent overseas in the employ of their country. Frances would eventually write many of her husband's subsequent western films, usually using the manly name, "Frank M. Carson."

His career in films got started when a bit player failed to show up for a part in a movie his wife was directing, *Just Around the Corner*, and he stepped in to take his place. Thomson had decided early on to pursue a career in Westerns, and recognized the importance of selecting the right horse. He purchased a dapple-gray hunter, and christened him, Silver-King.

Thomson then methodically began his plan to become a western star. He moved next door to famed comedian Harold Lloyd and stabled Silver King at Hoot Gibson's stables. He honed his craft by taking small film roles and training Silver King, so they would be ready when the time came. Thomson's rigid religious background more than likely gave him the motivation he needed to never waver from his plan. Never, up until that time, had anyone devised with such precision and skill a plan to become a western movie star!

By the mid-twenties, Westerns were thriving and producers were looking for stars to sign on for the huge slate of western films being produced. Thomson was ready to step up and become one of those stars. Producer Harry Joe Brown notice Thomson, in one of his small film roles, and signed him as his new cowboy star in the summer of 1923. Brown would release these films through Monogram Pictures (not the Monogram of the 1930s). The agreement called for six modestly budgeted films to be produced at the average of one every five weeks. Each film would cost $10,000, of which Thomson would receive $300 per week plus 5% of the profits. This was almost unheard of at that time, especially for a brand new star! The deal further stipulated that Thomson would get a $500 raise and 10% of the profits for the next set of films if the first six were successful. The films were indeed successful.

It's been said that, due to Thomson's immediate success, he opened the Hollywood gates for a new crop of cowboy stars. Tom Tyler, Bob Steele, Bob Custer, Wally Wales, Rex Bell, Buddy Roosevelt, Buffalo Bill, Jr. and Tim McCoy, to name a few, all came riding in on the popularity of Fred Thomson.

But Thomson's early Westerns were patterned after those of the first western superstar, Tom Mix. Adventure, daring stunts, and light comedy were Mix's stock in trade and Thomson followed this formula.

Harry Joe Brown eventually closed up shop and Thomson moved to Universal for a series, before being signed by Joseph P. Kennedy, father of our future president and attorney general, for his production company Film Booking Offices (FBO). FBO would eventually be the home of many other western stars including: Tom Tyler and Bob Steele. The studio would eventually become RKO where stars like George O' Brien, Tom Keene, Robert Mitchum, and Tim Holt would ride the range.

By the time he was signed by FBO, Thomson was the highest paid western star, making $10,000 per week and his own production company. Even Silver King had a contract plus a $100,000 life insurance policy. By 1926, Thomson was the number two box-office attraction. He would remain as such through 1927.

Even though Thomson was arguably the most popular western star at the time the studios, then as now, only look at the price tag; Thomson's was beginning to outweigh his popularity.

In 1928 Kennedy would sign Thomson's biggest competition for the cowboy hero throne, Tom Mix. By this time Thomson's production company was being paid $85,000, from which he would pay all production costs. With Mix now in the studio fold the handwriting was on the wall for Fred Thomson. He tried to sign with Paramount, but Kennedy refused to let him out of his contract. When his contract expired, Thomson immediately signed with Paramount Pictures. His contract with Paramount called for him to receive $250,000 per film, which would include his paycheck, which now amounted to $100,000 per film.

Paramount, unlike FBO, was a major studio and could well afford a star like Fred Thomson, but they couldn't help but notice that the independent studios were raking in the money with lower budget westerns, starring popular stars like Buck Jones, who was making movies for $4,000 per film and his main rival, Tom Mix working for a surprisingly low $7,500!

Paramount decided to create their very own western star. They found him in a fairly well known athlete of the time by the name of Vincent Markowski. They signed Markowski for only $75.00 per week and the ploy worked! He would get a raise in a year's time to $175. The new star's films were being produced for only $10,000 per film. Markowski's films delivered an audience at a difference of $240,000 between one of his films and one of Thomson's. Markowski's future seemed bright. His star would last through the thirties and into the forties. He would switch from good guy to bad guy with ease as he took on more character parts, even creating some memorable superheroes for the serials. You're probably scratching your heard and saying, "Wait a minute! I've never heard of Vincent Markowski." You're right! Markowski changed his name to Tom Tyler.

Paramount wasn't through, however, with Fred Thomson. They had the most popular western star and they weren't about to let him go. He had been the number two most popular star of '26 and '27 and might have reached number one in 1928 if tragedy hadn't struck Thomson once again. Thomson became seriously ill while working on the Paramount film *Jesse James*. A few days before Christmas he began limping, suffering from intense pain. Rushed to the hospital, it was found that he had a fever of 104 degrees. First diagnosed with kidney stones, it was later discovered that he was suffering from tetanus he had contracted from a nail scratch he received while working at his stable. The discovery was too late and the misdiagnoses cost Fred Thomson his life. He died on Christmas Day, 1928. He was only 38 years old. His pallbearers included: Harold Lloyd, silent matinee idol Charles Farrell, Douglas Fairbanks, and director George W. Hill, with Buster Keaton, and movie mogul Joseph M. Schenk as honorary pallbearers.

His widow, Frances Marion, would continue writing movies, winning Oscars for *The Big House* (1930) and *The Champ* (1931). She married George W. Hill, one of Fred's pallbearers, in 1930 and divorced him in 1933, one year before he committed suicide. She died in May 1973 after a long career as a writer and director.

Fred Thomson had all the ingredients that could have made him a popular star in the sound era, maybe even more so than Mix, Jones, Gibson, McCoy, Maynard and Tom Tyler. His career lasted less than a decade, but he made more than 30 films plus one serial, *The Eagle's Talon*. He is a true western star who deserves to be mentioned with the likes of Tom Mix and the rest who I have just mentioned. He is a true pioneer in the western genre.

While Fred Thomson is an almost forgotten superstar of silent Westerns, Leo Maloney is one of the forgotten pioneers of the sound Western. While not in the same class as Fred Thomson or the "Big Five," Maloney was a fairly popular silent western star, producer, and director.

Making his film debut in 1914, he starred in a series of films and serials for the Mutual Film Corp until 1920.

His big opportunity came when he signed with Pathe Films, where he began producing, directing, and writing his own films. Maloney had one small problem. He liked the bottle a bit too much. This would eventually be his downfall.

Leo definitely made a recognizable name for himself in silent films, but with the coming of "talkies" he had a plan to make his star shine even brighter, and it could have worked. If nothing else, it would have given him a firm place in the history of sound film. But fate would take a hand and cause Leo to become nothing more than a footnote. Before we talk about Leo, let's take a brief look at the advent of sound on film.

One of the big threats to sound films, and Westerns in particular, was how to utilize all the awkward equipment needed in the new medium. The stationary use of microphones and the whirring noise of the camera were eventually covered up by enclosing the camera, and cameraman, in a soundproof enclosure. This caused problems with breathing. Many times a cameraman would pass out from heat and lack of oxygen. Western film producers were concerned with the logistics of creating an action packed film under these circumstances, especially the problem the outside heat might have on the poor cameraman in the enclosure.

Eventually, creating an enclosure that would simply fit around the camera to muffle the noise solved these problems. Independent producers soon realized that the low-budget Western was actually the most economical "talkie" to shoot. Interior lighting could be kept to a minimum, in some cases simply putting up walls to resemble an interior, using the sun, and reflectors, to simulate indoor lighting.

Many studios hired stage actors in order to take advantage of their trained voices. Actors who had been successful in the silents would either adapt or fall by the wayside. Studios would hire diction coaches to help with the process. This made actors sound phony and effeminate in some cases. Many early talkies became talk-fests that don't hold up today. The stationary microphones required were generally hidden in some prop on the set; flower vases were very popular. This caused actors to have limited movement in order to stay near the microphone. If you've ever seen the classic musical, *Singing in the Rain*, which is all about this dilemma, you know what I mean.

Early on it was discovered that low budget Westerns could quickly be churned out without such problems. In early sound Westerns, sound could be kept to a minimum, or not used in some scenes at all. Thundering hooves or gunshots could be added later. Sometimes the sound was left out altogether making it appear that the horses might be wearing loafers. Dialogue was kept to a bare minimum to make way for lots of action. "Oaters" could cheaply, and quickly, be cranked out at one or two per week while making an easy profit. Running time was generally kept to less than an hour. Although the independents would thrive in the world of sound film, it would be a major studio that showed the way for producers of early sound Westerns.

By early '29, Fox was very aggressive in the advancement of sound. They produced a Western based on a story by O. Henry (William Sydney Porter) called *"The Caballero's Way."* The film would be called *In Old Arizona*, and it introduced one of the most enduring characters of western film, the "Cisco Kid." Popular, but non-Hispanic, actor Warner Baxter played the "Kid."

Actor/director Raoul Walsh was set to direct and play the title role, but when he lost an eye in an accident the role went to Baxter. Walsh settled on directing, while Baxter would win an Academy Award ® for his role. He would reprise the role twice in *The Arizona Kid* (1930) and *The Cisco Kid* (1931).

Fox proved that a major studio could successfully produce a sound Western, followed by Paramount who quickly released *The Virginian*, based on the popular novel by Owen Wister. The film starred up and coming actor Gary Cooper, and was directed by Victor Fleming. It too proved to be a success.

Between the releases of these two major sound films there was another sound western film produced and released, and the man behind it was Leo Maloney. Gathering together as much money as he could, Maloney slyly "borrowed' un-used equipment, and gathered up unexposed film stock (the "ends" as they are known) discarded during editing and left on the cutting room floor. In this way he produced *Overland Bound*, starring himself and Jack Perrin.

The film was crude in every way, but the fans enjoyed it, and the critics were kind in recognizing what could be done on a virtually non-existent budget. It appeared that Maloney had hit pay dirt with his movie, the first independent sound Western. Presidio Pictures, a small releasing company, released the picture and it did quite well. It was a time for celebration and Maloney certainly did, a bit too hard. While throwing a party, and drinking a bit too heavily, Maloney died from a heart attack. He was 41 years old.

Overland Bound should not only be recognized as the first independent sound Western in film history, but also the second sound Western produced at all! With his sudden death, Leo Maloney's hopes for success were dashed. Today most film historians recognize *The Virginian* as the second sound Western, but Leo Maloney was there beforehand.

By 1930, film companies were trying to figure out bigger and better ways of getting their films into the theaters, to stay in the forefront. M-*G*-M, and director King Vidor, quickly went into production with a sweeping outdoor production of *Billy the Kid* (1930) starring University of Alabama halfback, Johnny Mack Brown. It was filmed in a new wide-screen process known as Realife.

Fox and Raoul Walsh tried to repeat the success of *In Old Arizona* with another major Western called *The Big Trail* (1930). Walsh wanted Tom Mix to play the lead, but he was unavailable. Walsh hired a fresh young actor, a protégé of John Ford's, to play the lead. The actor, Duke Morrison (real name Marion Morrison) would take the name of John Wayne and become an icon. For the moment, however, he was a small time supporting player, who had been moving props and working as a gofer for Tom Mix and Ford.

Like *Billy the Kid*, *The Big Trail* used the gimmick of a wide screen process. The 55 mm format called "Fox Grandeur" was a failure, due in part to the wide screen process requiring theater owners to install special equipment. During the days of the depression theater owners were unable to afford the extra expense, and so the sweeping beautiful landscape of *The Big Trail* was lost on the regular theater screens of the '30s.

Gary Cooper was already an up and coming actor at the time of *The Virginian*, and went on to greater fame in short order.

Johnny Mack Brown would make a handful of films at M-G-M before being permanently relegated to B programmers for the rest of his career. He would stay in the Western top ten from 1940 through 1950, and is considered one of the greats of the genre.

It's been said that John Wayne's career would have paralleled Brown's if not for John Ford and *Stagecoach*. The Duke continued to struggle through films at Fox and Columbia without making much of a mark. He eventually drifted into oaters, supporting Buck Jones and Tim McCoy, and finally jumping from studio to studio in his own series of Westerns – Monogram's "Lone Star" series being the most popular.

When Monogram and Mascot, along with other small independents, reformed to create Republic Pictures, Wayne was considered one of the reliable cowboy stars. It would appear that his future would be in B Westerns. But his early friendship with Ford paid off.

The director offered him the role of the "Ringo Kid" and Wayne never had to look back. Brown never had a savior, like John Ford, to take him out of the 2nd feature category.

The success and Academy Award ® of *In Old Arizona*, and the success of other major features like *The Virginian* and *Billy the Kid*, not to mention the fame *The Big Trail* eventually achieved due to John Wayne's ascension into the ranks of super-stardom, has completely overshadowed the contribution Leo Maloney made to 'talkie' Westerns. Had Maloney lived maybe things would have been different...maybe not. But he did prove that low-budget independent Westerns could be extremely profitable, paving the way for such filmmakers as Victor Adamson AKA Denver Dixon, Ed Finney, William Pizor, and, probably the most successful, Harry "Pop" Sherman.

Both Fred Thomson and Leo Maloney deserve their place on the honor roll of western movie pioneers who did their part to popularize the art form. Hopefully, in some small way, this will help preserve their names.

Although my feelings are that Leo Maloney probably would have struggled in the independent field, Fred Thomson's story truly amazes me.

Not too long ago, a question about Thomson appeared in a Q & A column about movies and actors. The columnist had no idea who Fred Thomson was and tried to make it sound like there was never such a star! A quick trip to the Internet would have shown the so-called columnist that indeed Thomson existed, but it obviously wasn't important enough. What amazes me is that, although it has been almost eighty years since

Fred Thomson was a major star, he is rarely given credit in the history of western film. If he had lived to make "talkies" that might have been different. Here was a man who knew what he wanted and went for it, achieving stardom unheard of before the likes of Gene Autry in the era of sound. He was more powerful then any of the silent western stars, and most of the mainstream stars as well. To the "Big Five" of Mix, Maynard, McCoy, Gibson, and Jones should be added a sixth, Fred Thomson. To borrow a phrase from Yul Brynner in *The Ten Commandments*, "So let it be written—so let it be done."

Two pioneers of the western film. Ken Maynard and his horse, Tarzan, with former Fred Thomson director Al Rogell, attempting to try his hand at stuntwork. The shot was taken while Ken was working for First National.

Two pictures of Fred Thomson. The first is Fred with his horse, Silver King, and the second is of him directing his Paramount crew. Fred was the first western star to be given his own film crew.

Paramount would create their own western star with Vincent Markowski. However they would change his name to Tom Tyler. Tyler would have a successful career as both a hero and villain until arthritis stopped him.

Western movie pioneer Leo Maloney listens to Joe Rickson in a scene from "Two Gun of the Tumbleweed" (1927).

15

Leo looks concerned for Eileen Sedgwick (billed as Greta Yoltz) in a scene from "Yellow Contraband" (1928), again with Joe Rickson.

Leo Maloney (center) starting his "Overland Bound" tour. At his left, wearing the cap and pinstripe suit, with a big smile, is Leo's film cutter and future western film director Joe Kane.

*Joan Crawford and Johnny Mack Brown on the set of the early
sound film "Montana Moon" (1930). Note the size of the early
sound camera.*

*Note the size of the outdoor camera, circa 1936, used for this Ken
Maynard Columbia Western. Seated to the left of the camera are
director Spencer Bennet (legs crossed) and Ken Maynard.*

17

Hoot Gibson checks the sound on one of his early films for Universal Pictures.

The Different Faces of Tom Tyler
During The Sound Era

Tom Tyler as Kharis,
The Mummy's Hand (1940)

Tom as The Phantom (1943)

Considered by many to be the best serial ever produced:
The Adventures of Captain Marvel (1941)

The Three Mesquiteers
Tom Tyler, Rufe Davis, Bob Steele (1941-1942)

The Three Mesquiteers
Tom Tyler, Jimmy Dodd, Bob Steele (1942-1943)

20

CHAPTER TWO
MIXING IT UP WITH THE SHONTZ
BROTHERS
—or—
WHO WANTS TO DO MY STUNTS?

No other silent era film cowboy embodied the shape of things to come more than Tom Mix. From his fancy shirts, with angled pockets, to the tight-fitting pants, Tom was the western star who set the pace for all who followed, right down to his trick horse, Tony.

His background biography was also a combination of many exciting jobs that made him a natural hero for the silver screen. Tom was born in Texas, enlisted in the U.S. Army at 18, and served in the Spanish-American War as one of Teddy Roosevelt's Rough Riders. He was wounded during the Philippine Insurrection and rose to the rank of first sergeant. After his service years, Mix captured the notorious Schontz Brothers while serving as a U.S. Marshal. He later rode with the famed Miller Brothers' 101 Ranch Show. Anyone would agree that this was a truly exciting life. There's only one problem. Most of it is about as true as the daring do that Mix portrayed on the screen.

Mix, ever the showman, created a bio that would turn him into a hero off screen as well as on. It wasn't until years later that the truth became known to more than just a handful of people.

The truth is, Mix was not born in Texas, never was a Rough Rider, and never rose to the rank of first sergeant. What is true is that Mix served in the coast artillery during the Spanish-American War. In 1901, he signed up for a second hitch, but later deserted. He was never a U.S. Marshal, however he did serve as a city policeman in Dewey, Oklahoma for a short period, as well as a construction camp security guard.

What about his capturing the notorious Shontz Brothers? That alone would qualify Mix as a hero of gigantic proportions. Along with the James Gang, Billy the Kid, and Butch Cassidy, the Shontz Brothers stand tall as renegades of the first order. This would be the crowning achievement of his law career, if...well...if the Shontz Brothers existed. But they didn't. They were another fabrication from the mind of Tom Mix.

One thing that is true is that he signed with the Miller Brothers' 101 Ranch Show. Not as a star, but as a "Safety Man." This was indeed a dangerous job, which consisted of making sure that the wild animals were diverted from harming the cast and crew.

Mix came to films in 1910 working as a wrangler and bit player for the Selig Polyscope Company. Finally, in 1914, he was given his own starring series for Selig Polyscope, starting with *The Real Thing In Cowboys.*

Although Mix started in movies before William S. Hart, it took time for him to catch on. In 1917, Mix signed with Fox Studios. It was while under contract to Fox that a formula was created for Mix and his Westerns. The studio based Mix's stunt packed movies on the popular athletic films of Douglas Fairbanks. Fairbanks had become a hit with film adaptations of Robin Hood, Zorro, and the Thief of Bagdad. Fox decided to turn Mix into a hero who would defy gravity, an action hero who took his job lightly.

Up until then audiences where enthralled with the sober, and authentically detailed stories that William S. Hart displayed on the screen. It didn't matter that Hart's background was more from William Shakespeare than Zane Grey. Hart's carefully crafted saga's where honorable efforts that carried Broncho Billy's good-bad guy character to further extremes, many times with not so happy results.

The one mainstay ingredient that Hart introduced to western films was the trusty, reliable horse. The B western heroes who became popular always had an identifiable horse, the one thing they could always depend on. Fritz was Hart's contribution. Mix would take that one step further and create the first horse with a personality. Tony was that horse. Fred Thomson recognized this when he went looking for his "personality" horse, which was to become Silver King. Tarzan, Champion, Trigger, Topper, and KoKo would become just some of the mounts that would become associated with the stars that rode them.

Other identifiable facets of the B western cowboy also showed up first in the Mix Westerns. The fancy tight pants and shirts, which displayed symbolized shirt pockets distinctive to each star where first worn by Mix. This couldn't have been easy for Hart to understand. It wasn't authentic or practical. If anything it was a bit of an effeminate idea. But it stuck!

This was also during a time when the real "Wild West" was still fresh in peoples' minds. Real icons of the west, like Wyatt Earp and Bat Masterson were still alive to recount their exploits. It must have amused them to see how the heroes of the west were already being given a revisionist history. They themselves would be given this type of whitewashing with time, but they also helped it to happen with their own versions of their histories.

The "dude duds" that would become a mainstay, especially with the cowboy stars at Republic Pictures, were impractical. Any "real cowboy" who would show up at a rodeo, let alone for ranch work, dressed like that would have been laughed at or possibly beaten to a pulp by the other cowhands. But, if you were a B cowboy movie star, you were greeted with open arms. It was accepted, although not really believed, by every man, woman, and child who would greet the next Gene Autry, Roy Rogers, or Rex Allen film to come down the trail. These heroes weren't part of the real world, so it was okay. Later on this revisionist view would be carried even further, when Gene or Roy would be thrown into a Western featuring Champion or Trigger chasing down some crook or saboteur driving a high-speed car or truck through the "Wild West."

So, while stars like Hoot Gibson preferred more practical duds, stars like Ken Maynard, and even an authentic cowpoke like Tim McCoy, embraced the new styles that would reach it's peak during the years of World War II with the big budget musical adventures of Roy Rogers.

One of the great legends about old Tom is that he performed all his own stunts. It's now known that other people were used to double him for many of his more difficult stunts.

Director Lambert Hillyer once said of Mix, *"Tom carried a complete stock company of cowboys, from cook to wranglers, and they all doubled for him at times. However this was considered top-secret and not one of his employees admitted this fact to a stranger. Sometimes, however, if he didn't like the way a stunt looked, he'd get sore and do it over himself."*

Not many people realize that, in the days before special effects, sharpshooters off camera used live ammunition. Lambert went on to say, *"I spread lead around him*

(Mix) in picture after picture with him always yelling: 'Come closer!' Mix was himself a good man with a rifle, rope, or six-gun. Very fast on the draw, and, as a stagecoach driver, one of the best."

Mix is a prime example of how to use the press to further, what could have been, a very ordinary film career. He had charisma and a knack for self-promotion. He was the first to display the talents that were essential in creating a lasting western film star.

Tom Mix's career lasted from 1914 until 1935. His final film, actually a serial, *The Miracle Rider* was for Nat Levine's Mascot Pictures. It was Mix himself who decided to call it quits. It would be the same year that Levine would consolidate his studio with other small independents, including Monogram, to create Republic Pictures. Along with Herbert J. Yates, Levine would open up the B western movie genre with the creation of Republic. Ironically, Ken Maynard would leave Levine in a huff around the same time. Two of the "Big Five" from the previous decade missed out on being members of the greatest western film studio of the next twenty years.

In 1936 the first Motion Picture Herald Poll came out announcing the top ten western stars. Of the stars who entered film during the silent era, Buck Jones came in at number one, Ken Maynard at number five, Tim McCoy at number eight, and Hoot Gibson at number nine. The other spots were filled by George O' Brien, another hold-over from silent film, at number two, Gene Autry at number three, and another silent star, with a new lease on life, William Boyd at number four. Singing cowboy Dick Foran held the number six position, John Wayne was number seven and Buster Crabbe came in at number ten. Of the

"Big Five" only Mix was nowhere to be found.

If Mix had continued in film, he might have had the same success the other "Big Five" had in talkies. Instead, he decided to ride away while he was still able to and keep his legend intact. Of all those who started in the days of the silent Westerns, Mix stands alone as a symbol of what was to come. The flashy clothes, dynamic demeanor, and Tony, his wonder horse, opened the way for Gene, Roy and most of those to follow in the world of B Westerns.

He had been used to an extravagant life-style, but with four ex-wives making demands his money was dwindling quickly. He decided to give motion pictures another try. The sixty year old Mix was soon to find that he had been away too long. Visiting his old director, John Ford, Mix told him that he needed a job. Ford, now one of the most successful directors in the business, had no work for him. Nor did producer Sol Wurtzel at 20th Century Fox. The very people he had made millions of dollars for now had no use for him.

Shortly afterwards, on October 12, 1940, while traveling on Highway 79 (between Florence and Oracle, Arizona), Mix's Cord convertible failed to negotiate a sharp turn. An aluminum suitcase, on the back deck of the car, was thrown forward breaking his neck. A western film icon had passed on. A monument was erected at the spot of the accident which reads: *"In Memory of Tom Mix, whose spirit left his body on this spot, and whose characterization, and portrayals in life served to better fix memories of the old west in the minds of living men."* It is a testament to his true value as a western star that the monument still stands where his life ended.

Tom Mix, the first western film superstar, ready for action . . . .

. . . and here he is in action!

The Tom Mix monument, where it all ended October 12, 1940.

CHAPTER THREE
WHO WAS THE FIRST
SINGING COWBOY?
—or—
OUT WITH THE OLD AND IN
WITH THE NEW

Former Sons of the Pioneers member Rusty Richards once tried to stump me by asking who the first singing cowboy movie star was? I knew he wanted me to say Gene Autry, but I knew it wasn't so. I looked him straight in the eye and said, "Why, it was Ken Maynard." He looked surprised, and then admitted that I was right.

Ken Maynard is credited with being the first of the cowboy stars to use singing in his movies. From 1929 through 1934, Ken could be found playing the banjo, guitar, and occasionally the fiddle, as he sang, although not exceptionally well, through a number of films starting with *The Wagon Master* for Universal.

He also became the first to have a recording contract, starting with a simple rendition of "Home on the Range" for American Record Corporation. In September of 1930, Ken recorded eight songs for the Columbia Graphophone Company, but only two of the songs, "The Cowboy's Lament," and "The Lone Star Trail" was ever released.

Ken also wrote some of his songs as well, such as "The Cattle Drive," and "Wheels of Destiny." Although singing cowboys would star in many films using popular song titles Ken was the first. He appeared in Universal's *The Strawberry Roan* in 1933. Gene Autry would appear in a film with the same title and song in 1948. It would be his first film for Columbia Pictures.

Maynard was an innovator, who reinvented his self with the coming of sound. Also, like Mix, he tried to pass himself off as a Texan. In actuality, he was born in Vevay, Indiana, not Mission, Texas as his bio stated.

His career started in 1923 with a bit part in *The Man Who Won*, and ended in 1944 with *Harmony Trail*. The film, which was re-released in 1947 as *White Stallion*, also featured Eddie Dean, Max Terhune and his dummy Elmer, and a minor yet interesting western actor by the name of Rocky Camron.

As with many of the actors in this book much of the information you can find about Camron is incorrect. Many biographies state that he was born Gene Alsace, but the truth is that he was born Rockford G. Camron, not Gene Alsace nor Rockford Cane Camron, as other bios claim. It is also claimed that his screen name came from an amalgam of Allan "Rocky" Lane and Rod Cameron. This can't be true for some very simple reasons. First, it's obvious that he was using the Rocky Camron name by 1944 and Allan Lane didn't add the "Rocky" nickname to his billing until 1947. Secondly, Rod Cameron certainly wouldn't have been a role model since he was just coming into his own as a western star in the mid 1940s.

The truth about Camron is that he started out as Tim McCoy's stunt-double before taking on bit parts under the name Gene Alsace; not exactly a superstar quality name! Later he would change his name to "Buck Coburn," and finally Rocky Camron, which he would sometimes spell as "Cameron." He had some small success in bottom of the barrel westerns, but nothing of great importance. Actually, his continual insistence of changing his name probably didn't help his audience identification either. This would be Tom Keene's problem, when he couldn't decide whether he was Tom Keene or Tom Powers!

Meanwhile, back to Maynard. Old Ken had started the ball rolling for singing cowboys with the advent of talking pictures. But his major contribution to the musical western, and B westerns in general, wasn't due to his singing prowess. Actually it probably had nothing to do with him at all, but a decision forced upon him by the power brokers at the studio soon to be known as Republic Pictures.

His 1934 film, *In Old Santa Fe*, would introduce the first honest to goodness singing cowboy film star, as well as the first official western film sidekick. Of course I'm talking about Gene Autry and Lester "Smiley" Burnette. Frankie Marvin, a fellow Oklahoma native and another member of Gene's musical group would appear in some early Autry outings, but would find musical success behind the scenes. Two of his best-known compositions are "Cowboy's Heaven," and "It's a Sin."

Given a few simple numbers in their first film Gene and Smiley were more or less glorified extras, but Gene's easy-going style, and Smiley's clowning, and musical expertise made them a hit with producer Nat Levine. This may have peeved Maynard just a bit!

The thing that probably set Maynard off more than anything was the fact that Levine had Maynard's own singing in the film dubbed! Imagine being the daddy of the singing cowboy in films and then have a producer deem your singing not suitable, but instead hire an honest to goodness singer to sing in your film.

31

Levine probably had one miserable cowpoke on his hands in the form of Ken Maynard. After all, this was Maynard's first film under his exclusive contract with Levine and Mascot Pictures. Gene and Smiley would again appear with Maynard in his next project for Mascot, a serial called *Mystery Mountain* (1934).

Maynard was then set to star in another serial, *The Phantom Empire* (1935). But Ken, possibly feeling that he was being used to groom Gene, decided to break his contract with Mascot. With Maynard gone, Levine moved Gene up to the star position in the serial and Smiley as, of course, his sidekick. The rest, as they say, is history. Did Levine use Autry as leverage against Maynard? Was the whole idea of bringing Gene in possibly a ploy on the part of Levine to get out of his contract with the difficult star?

Maynard's wild ways were a bit of a difficulty for the studio, and the use of Gene might have been Levine's way of saying that they could go on without him. Maynard, no longer the draw that he had been during the days of silent film and the early '30s, though still a "name" to be reckoned with, was living well beyond his drawing power by 1934. Woman, and alcohol were his downfall. Mascot refused to put up with his demands when they recognized that they could build up a newcomer like Gene Autry into a homegrown star for the studio. When Gene Autry became a star he revolutionized and revitalized the B western. It would cause a prolonged death-knell for the silent western stars still trying to act as if they were the young heroes they had been once upon a time. The smart ones, like Harry Carey, became successful character actors. The unwise, like Maynard, continued to live on past glories, even while the expanse of his waist-size approached and surpassed that of his ego.

Levine, later in his life, was quoted as saying that he didn't see much star quality in Gene Autry. However, he must have seen something in him. Levine might have figured that using him in a couple of Maynard films might help the young performer develop a style. Like Maynard, Gene Autry developed more into an on screen personality then a true actor. He had that certain "IT" that would sustain him, despite his obvious lack of thespian talent.

Little did Levine know that Autry would also eventually become a royal pain to Republic Pictures. By that time he was the biggest cowboy star ever and the studio needed him. Unlike Maynard, Autry's star never descended.

Beginning with Gene Autry, Republic established the rules that they would, more or less, follow into the early '50s. They would nurture their own talent. Roy Rogers, although he did appear with the Sons of the Pioneers at Columbia and Republic, was the first sensation after Gene Autry. Tailor-made stars like Sunset Carson, Monte Hale and Rex Allen would follow.

Others like Don Barry and Allan Lane had been featured by other studios before their move to Republic but not as western stars. A major exception was the popular William Elliott who made the move from melodrama to Westerns at Columbia Pictures before moving to Republic. Other stars like Bob Steele, Tom Tyler, and Robert Livingston, would pass through Republic's gates while appearing for studios like PRC and the newly reformed Monogram. Barry and Carson would also star for lesser studios by the early 1950s, while Hale would take smaller roles in other stars' films and television programs.

In the early years, aside from Smiley Burnette, sidekicks were seasoned film veterans like George Hayes, and Al St. John. Although they weren't considered sidekicks, but more a form of comedy relief to pad out a film or a quick way to explain important plot points without taking too much screen time, they became an important part of the programmer Westerns. Later on, Republic Pictures would vary the system by trying out sidekicks who had made their name in other areas of show business. Actors/ performers like Sterling Holloway, Buddy Ebsen, Carl "Alfalfa" Switzer, Andy Devine, Gordon Jones, Guinn "Big Boy" Williams, and Pinky Lee tried their hand at "sidekickery" with varying degrees of success.

By 1935, the old western stars like Maynard, Hoot Gibson, Tim McCoy, and Buck Jones were still making movies, but their glory days were over. They were replaced by younger stars like John Wayne, George O' Brien, Tom Tyler and Bob Steele, among others.

Aside from Wayne, the younger stars I've just mentioned had earned popularity in the silent era, but gained momentum in the early thirties. George O' Brien, like Tyler and Steele, would peak by the early '40s. The three would eventually lend support to John Wayne in different projects when he became a major star.

Singing cowboys came by the truckload post-Autry. They all wanted to cash in on the Gene Autry craze. Most of them fell by the wayside. Some, like Tex Ritter, or to a lesser extent Dick Foran, and Fred Scott had a fair run, but no studio but Republic could produce a long lasting singing cowboy. Toward the end of the '30s, Gene would pave the way for Roy.

By the next decade the competition thinned out a bit. Monte Hale gave it a good college try, until they found a true singing cowboy in Rex Allen. Eddie Dean was very successful for PRC in the Roy and Rex "I can act mold," and Jimmy Wakely in the Gene Autry "personality rather than an actor mold" at Monogram. But these studios didn't have the clout that Republic did.

Still, nobody gave Maynard the credit for being the first. Unlike Mix, Gibson, McCoy, or Jones, Maynard tried to re-invent himself as a singing cowboy. He recognized the possibilities that sound could afford, and he was ready to make use of the "talkies."

Unfortunately the studios didn't care. The "Big Five," singing or not, were expendable. In the end they helped the marquee value of many poverty row studios that could get them cheap. Tom Mix turned his back on films while the getting was good, and Jones died tragically in the 1942 Cocoanut Grove fire in Boston. But Gibson, McCoy, and Maynard held in there. By the time they hung up their guns they were definitely interchangeable, playing roles in "Three Mesquiteer" knock-offs like "The Trail Blazers," and "Rough Riders" Ken Maynard retired from series film work in the late 40s, but he continued to make appearances at fairs and rodeos. When he passed away, on March 27, 1973, he was broke, an alcoholic, and living in a trailer. He was 75. It was common knowledge that Gene Autry took care of Maynard during his latter years, but never took any credit for it. Nothing, however, can take away the fact that, out of the top five cowboy stars of the silent era, Maynard took better advantage of the new era of sound. He was a true pioneer of the Western genre.

As a side-note, Bob Steele also did a musical western, *The Oklahoma Cyclone*, for Trem Carr and Tiffany Pictures. Released August 8, 1930, the film was the first in a proposed musical series that never took off. It was later remade as Tex Ritter's first starring film for Grand National, *Song of the Gringo* (1936).

By introducing musical numbers to the Western genre, Ken Maynard got the ball rolling. Then, by having newcomer Gene Autry appear in one film and a serial with him, even if he wasn't too happy about it, he created the star who would make the singing cowboy a viable artform.

So the next time anybody asks you who the first singing cowboy of the silver screen was? Look 'em straight in the eye and say, "Ken Maynard." And if they don't believe you, tell them to buy my book and find out for themselves!

Ken Maynard poised to sing and relaxing on his horse, Tarzan

Trailblazers Maynard (center) and Hoot Gibson (left), two of the 'Big Five' of the silent movies, are seen here watching the youngster of the group, Bob Steele, as he thrashes George Chesebro circa 1944. Maynard and Gibson didn't like working with Steele, feeling that he stole their thunder.

Here are two more of the "Big Five," Buck Jones (center, holding the gun) and Colonel Tim McCoy (on the stairs holding the gun). Sidekick favorite, Raymond Hutton, is holding the gun to the left in this 1941 production shot.

37

Publicity sheet for Bob Steele's early musical Western, "The Oklahoma Cyclone." The film was released on August 8, 1930, and featured eight songs, five of which were sung by Steele. This is believed to possibly be the first in a proposed musical series. Steele would do two more, with fewer songs than this one. He never did another musical Western of his own. The film was remade in 1936 as "Song of the Gringo," starring Tex Ritter. Steele's brother, Bill Bradbury is said to have done the singing for John Wayne when he portrayed "Singing Sandy."

CHAPTER FOUR
THE MYSTERY OF "SINGING SANDY"
—or—
WHAT WERE THEY THINKING?

If you've ever seen the "Singing Sandy" Saunders movie, *Riders of Destiny*, you have to scratch your head and wonder, "What the heck were they thinkin' of?"

Can you imagine someone actually pitching this idea? "Hey, we're gonna take a B western movie actor, how about John Wayne? And we'll put him on a horse, give him a guitar, and have him sing. Oh, we know Wayne can't sing, let alone play the guitar, so we'll have someone sing and play for him. It'll be great! A real boffo hit! We'll make a whole series of these and we'll call him 'Singing Sandy!'"

The first question that comes to mind has to be, "Why not get somebody who can actually sing and play the guitar?"

Was the result as embarrassing to watch back then as it is now? Probably not, in light of the fact that in the mid-30s the Duke wasn't the icon that he is now. Nevertheless, I imagine it still would have been awkward.

When Jolson spoke in *The Jazz Singer* a Pandora's box was opened. Studios scurried to equip themselves for the next "craze" called "talkies."

Once the dust settled, Westerns proved to be a quick and cheap way to make a buck. By the early '30s, there were more western stars than you could shake a stick at. Ken Maynard opened up the door for the possibility of a singing cowboy in the movies, and producer Paul Malvern decided to capitalize on it. Malvern had signed John Wayne to a series of Westerns for his Monogram "Lone Star" series.

The public liked the young action western star, and, after

he left Warner Bros., he went right into the extremely low budget Lone Star efforts. These low budget "oaters" would place Wayne in the running for the most popular western star of the early 30s; but his first one for Malvern, as Singing Sandy, could have easily been his swan song. Paul Malvern had the idea of turning Wayne into a singing cowboy. There were only a couple of obstacles to overcome. John Wayne couldn't sing nor play the guitar. The answer to the problem was simple. Get somebody to sing and play the guitar for him. Wayne was already a popular western mainstay by this time, so the recognition factor was there. Another thing to consider is that, in the early days of talking pictures, the studios were liable to try anything to make a buck. Having a recognizable star like John Wayne on screen, and have somebody else sing for him, may have seemed like a logical thing to do at the time.

Many fans believe that there was more than one Singing Sandy film produced; in actuality there was only one. The film was *Riders of Destiny* released in 1933, thus making Wayne the second official singing cowboy to hit the silver screen after Ken Maynard, even though Bob Steele had dabbled in singing as well. It's fun to watch John Wayne on his horse, or serenading his leading lady Celia Parker, all the while trying to make us believe that he can actually play the guitar and sing. It didn't work and the fans of the time didn't buy the premise.

His next film, *Sagebrush Trail* (1933), was back in the usual Wayne groove, and "Singing Sandy" Saunders would soon be a memory that would occasionally come back to haunt Wayne. The Duke would later say that he felt like a pansy playing the part, so the film shows just how well he could handle himself, even at that early stage of his career, in a part he felt demeaning.

In 1935, as Monogram was making the changeover to Republic Pictures, the Duke was once again caught singing, again with guitar in hand, in *Westward Ho*. The result wasn't any less embarrassing.

Who really sang for John Wayne as Singing Sandy? Buck Taylor, Newly on *Gunsmoke*, told me that Glenn Strange, who played Sam the Bartender on the long running TV western, claimed that he did the singing for John Wayne. It could have been true. Strange was a fixture in many Westerns of the '30s and '40s. He was also an excellent singer and accomplished songwriter. But it wasn't him. He may have dubbed Wayne's warbling in *Westward Ho*. Strange does appear in that movie, as does actor/singer Jack Kirk, who has also been credited as doing the singing for Singing Sandy.

Many say that it was Smith Ballew. Ballew was a pleasant enough singer, who appeared in five Westerns in '37 and '38. His films were the only western series ever produced by Twentieth Century-Fox. He was capable and handsome, reminding one of Randolph Scott or Gary Cooper. He also appeared on the 1938 Motion Picture Herald Poll of western stars at number eight, between Bob Steele and Tex Ritter respectively. But, although he gained a following as a popular vocalist, orchestra leader, and recording artist, he never clicked at the box-office. To set the record straight, Ballew wasn't the voice for Singing Sandy either.

Bill Bradbury, brother of Bob Steele and son of famed Westerns director Robert N. Bradbury who directed *Riders of Destiny*, is the person officially credited as the man behind the Duke's warbling in the film. And so, the case is closed on the mystery of Singing Sandy. Unless, that is, there's positive proof that Strange, Ballew, or Kirk did the singing. Then again, maybe it was Ken Maynard? Naw, I don't think so.

John Wayne as "Singing Sandy" in "Riders of Destiny," with Celia Parker. This picture was taken during one of the Duke's moments without a guitar in his hand. Maybe he's pointing the gun at the prop man threatening to pull the trigger if he hands him a guitar, one more time.

"Singing Sandy"was the role devised for John Wayne by director-author Robert N. Bradbury. Bradbury (seated-pointing is directing a scene from "Blue Steel" (1934); Wayne is seen leaning against the hitching post.

John Wayne, with guitar in hand, leading a sing along in "Westward Ho." Glen Strange is seated far right, while Jack Kirk is seated directly to the left of the Duke.

Smith Ballew was the only cowboy star to ever be signed to a series by Twentieth Century Fox. He made five films for them, including: "Roll Along, Cowboy" (1937), with John Wayne's Singing Sandy leading lady, Cecilia Parker. Gordon Elliott was featured in the film. Elliott later found immense success in Westerns when he moved to Columbia Pictures and changed his name to William "Wild Bill" Elliott.

CHAPTER FIVE
TOO MANY BILLS
—or—
A MORTIFIED MULFORD MAKES MONEY

We've all been there. You know...too many bills. But, in the mid-1930s, it affected one film star in a most unusual way. William Boyd had been a successful motion picture star ever since Cecil B. DeMille took a liking to him. DeMille used Boyd in his movies, first as an extra and then helped Boyd catapult to fame as a leading man.

By the end of the 1920s, he had starred in some of the biggest films to come out of the silent era including: *The Volga Boatman* (1926), *Yankee Clipper* (1927), and *King of Kings* (1927), just to name a few. During this time he made one Western, *The Last Frontier* (1926).

With the coming of sound, Boyd was still very much in demand. His premature blondish silver hair and strong voice made him a strong contender for "talking pictures." He starred in such films as: *Officer O' Brien* (1930), *His First Command* (1930) and *The Painted Desert* (1931), in which a young Clark Gable played the villain.

William Boyd was living the good life. Known for his partying ways, however, it came as no surprise when his name and picture appeared in several newspapers connecting him to a gambling scandal. Overnight his career took a nosedive. Today this might help a career, but, in the strict 30s, a film audience wanted their stars squeaky clean. Studios hired publicity hacks whose responsibility was to keep any scandal out of the news. But it was too late to save Boyd. His picture had been plastered on papers throughout the nation. There was no way to save him or his career.

Nobody wanted another scandal like that of Roscoe "Fatty" Arbuckle. Arbuckle had been a beloved film comedian until his name had been dragged through the mud during a well-publicized rape/murder case. His successful career came crashing down around him. The studios, and the public, had already passed judgment on Arbuckle by the time the court found him innocent of the crime. How times have changed, when you consider this case alongside that of O.J. Simpson!

William Boyd might well have had thoughts about Arbuckle's downfall, for the same thing was happening to him. The problem was William Boyd, matinee idol, was innocent of the crime. Movie star William Boyd wasn't the "Bill" Boyd that was involved in the sordid scandal. However, his picture was immediately placed alongside the scandal story by the newspapers without any investigation into the matter. By the time a retraction was printed nobody noticed, nobody cared, and the damage was done.

To make matters worse, there weren't just two "Bill" Boyd's in show business at the time. There were three! Besides our hero, William Boyd the movie star, there was Bill Boyd the character actor and the guilty party, and Bill Boyd the western music performer.

Keep in mind that this was before the days of the Screen Actors Guild. One of the by-laws of S.A.G. is the rule stating that no two actors can have the same name and be in the union. Thus, a well-known British actor had to change his name from James Stewart to Stewart Granger, a young comedian/actor had to change his name from Michael Douglas to Michael Keaton, and Michael J. Fox had to add the "J" because there was another Michael Fox in the union, and the list goes on and on. But, in the early '30s, this wasn't the case.

Three Bill Boyd's may seem ridiculous now, but pre-S.A.G. it was nothing.

After the scandal, Bill Boyd, the guilty character actor, would change his name to Bill "Stage" Boyd, and the western performer Bill Boyd would go by Bill "Cowboy Rambler" Boyd, and sometimes Bill "Radio" Boyd. Confusion would come into play once again when Bill "Cowboy Rambler" Boyd would star in a series of Westerns for Producers Releasing Corporation (PRC) in the early 1940s but, by that time, William Boyd was so firmly entrenched in people's minds as Hopalong Cassidy he didn't need to worry.

Originally, William Boyd was set to play another role in the first "Hoppy" film *Hop-A-Long Cassidy* (1935), (also known as *Hopalong Cassidy Enters*). His career had fallen so far that the best he could do, to stay in the film business, was to take a subordinate role in an independent western film. But fortune smiled on Boyd when the star of the picture James Gleason, the trainer in *Here Comes Mr. Jordan*, backed out of playing Cassidy due to a money dispute with producer Harry Sherman.

Independent producer Harry "Pop" Sherman had wisely arranged to have his Hoppy pictures released through Paramount Pictures to ensure greater coverage. He needed a star quickly. Boyd saw his chance and approached Sherman about the possibility of playing Cassidy. Boyd's power of persuasion worked. Possibly using his past fame, or notoriety, as a springboard Boyd convinced Sherman to place him in the lead role. Not everyone was happy with this decision, especially Cassidy creator Clarence E. Mulford.

Mulford's creation was closer in design to that of the originally intended star James Gleason, although the written character was in his 20s. The slight, limping, red-headed, tobacco spitting, ornery young cuss from Mulford's books and stories was replaced with the sleek, silver-blond, older, dashing figure dressed in the soon-to-be familiar dark outfit. Of course the outfit would be a concession to the flamboyant western-wear already becoming pervasive in the B western film world. Later, Boyd would try to alter the "Hoppy" look, but was unsuccessful.

The Cassidy series achieved a couple of firsts in the western film genre. It was the first time George Hayes was to play a continuing sidekick character in a series. Although Hayes had played in numerous Westerns, most notably with John Wayne, he had never actually been paired with the hero on a continuing basis.

George appeared alongside Boyd in August of '35, in one of the first full- blown western series. However, he didn't play "Windy" the character he became known for in the Cassidy series. Instead he played a character by the name of "Uncle Ben."

Smiley Burnette would appear as the character "Frog Millhouse" in his first series film with Gene Autry in September of '35. The film was *Tumbling Tumbleweeds*, which also featured George Hayes. So technically, although Hayes beat Burnette into series work by one month, old Smiley beat George out in playing a regular character in a series.

As stated, by the time Sherman cast George Hayes in his western series, the veteran actor was already making a name for himself in Westerns. "Pop" Sherman knew this and wanted Hayes in his pictures. Sherman hired him on a picture-by-picture basis without thinking of Hayes as a regular sidekick. He would play characters with names like "Uncle Ben," "Spike," and "Shanghai." By the fifth film, it was evident that George Hayes was a popular part of the Cassidy series.

Sherman permanently gave him the name Windy Halliday, a name he had used in the third entry of the series. It was also a name that Sherman made sure he kept when George Hayes moved over to Republic Pictures to join an up and coming western star by the name of Roy Rogers, forcing Hayes to come up with another nickname, thus "Gabby" was born.

Another groundbreaking first that came from the Hoppy films is that, it presented a trio of likable heroes in a continuing western series. The Three Mesquiteers would make this incredibly popular at Republic.

As the series evolved we would come to associate ourselves with either the firm, tough but goodhearted, brains of the group Hopalong Cassidy, the impetuous hotheaded romantic Johnny Nelson, Lucky Jenkins, Johnny Travers, Jimmy Rogers, etc., or the bumbling, but reliable, comic Windy Halliday or California Carlson.

William "Hoppy" Boyd would come to realize that his re-birth as a western star could be a mixed blessing. For the rest of his career Boyd would never be able to shake the image of Hopalong Cassidy. Never again did he play the dashing leading man in a biblical epic or drawing room drama.

But Boyd was a businessman and, like Gene Autry, he would come to realize that his career probably lasted longer than it would have otherwise. He would be a major hero of young and old for generations to come, well into his twilight years, when many of his peers were reduced to walk-ons in television programs or grade Z films.

The role of Hopalong Cassidy would overpower Boyd and cause him to change his ways and become an upstanding role model in his private life as well as on screen. But it would take some time. Robert Mitchum would start his career in small roles in the Hoppys, and had this to say about Boyd:

"William Boyd drank more than any man I ever saw; he kept quarts of whiskey on the set. He drained one every day."

Boyd was a strong contender for the most popular western star of the time. So popular would the character become that in 1974 Roy Rogers would record the hit song, "Hoppy, Gene, and Me," which would forever include William Boyd as one of the terrific trio of western film.

Beginning in 1936 and 1937 respectively, the Motion Picture Herald Poll and the Boxoffice Poll began polling theater exhibitors and moviegoers as to who were the top ten western stars. William Boyd made the lists from 1936 through 1950, never leaving the top five during all that time! He would reappear on the Motion Picture Herald Poll at number ten in 1952. This was the same year he started to shoot his television version of Hoppy, as well as appearing in full costume in the big budget movie, *The Greatest Show On Earth*, for former mentor Cecil B. DeMille.

One little-known fact about Bill Boyd is that he hated the dark blue/black costume that became so familiar with the fans. Whenever he could Boyd would trade the dark outfit for a lighter toned variant of the same costume, as he did throughout his 1940 - 41 Hopalong Cassidy films.

By the end of the 1943-44 season, Sherman decided to end the series. He had gone on to produce a series of Zane Grey adventures, with former Cassidy bit player Robert Mitchum among others. The Hoppy series had a good long run of nine seasons and fifty-four pictures. With no hopes of resurrecting a leading man career, Boyd went on the road doing live appearances as Hoppy.

Finally, in 1946, a group of investors wanted to finance a series of new Hoppy adventures. With the help of Bill Boyd, the investors were able to secure the rights from Sherman, who had continued to pay Mulford for the rights to the character despite his ending the series.

Sherman, ever the businessman, had retained the rights in hope of starting a new series of Hopalong Cassidy adventures with a new and much younger star. He also wanted to give Gene and Roy a run for their money and have the new "Hoppy" sing! Sherman approached Rex Allen, already making a name for himself, to see if he would be interested in bringing the new interpretation of "Hoppy" to the screen. Rex agreed, but nothing ever became of it.

Sherman, eventually got over the idea of bringing Hoppy back to the screen, and the timing of Boyd and his backers must have been right. Sherman not only sold the rights to Boyd and his group to make a new Hopalong Cassidy series, but he also sold the investors the rights to all but the first half dozen Hopalong Cassidy films he had made; he had already sold the rights to those first six films.

As Boyd began to re-tool the series, under the banner of William Boyd Productions, he kept himself busy on the road. It was during this time that a future western film icon was hired as Controller of the new production company. His name is Jack Elam.

As Elam tells it: *"I was with Bill Boyd for two years. We made six Hoppys a year. I wasn't a CPA but I was a public accountant, at Sam Goldwyn Studios, when I was recommended for the job with Boyd. At one point, Bill decided to take a rodeo to Hawaii and then move on to Australia. Nelson Eddy financed the tour for $125,000. We got over to Hawaii and the arena held 25,000 people. On opening day we had 2,500 people come to see us. The following night we had 1,800 and the next night 1,200. We pulled the plug on the tour and came back home."*

Despite the failed Hawaiian tour Boyd found great success with his new Hoppy series. In 1946, *The Devil's Playground* was released through United Artists. Sherman had started using U.A. instead of Paramount in 1942 starting with *Leather Burners*.

As a concession to himself, for now being in control of the Hoppy series, Boyd tried to change his character in subtle ways. He tested the waters of audience reaction by using a less flamboyant tan outfit, which bore no relation to the more familiar costume. It was a more traditional western shirt, pants and boot apparel, sometimes using the "dude" clothes he occasionally wore in earlier films to disguise his true identity. These were more to his liking, rather then the dark outfit imposed on him by Sherman. The actor knew his audience, however, and would never completely forsake the costume that had brought him so much fame and fortune.

Hoppy became a cash cow for Boyd. Between merchandise, in which his take was estimated at $25,000,000 in 1951 alone, personal appearances, and a radio program the once washed up actor was riding high.

In 1948, Boyd began selling the rights to television stations to show the older Sherman Hoppy films. By cutting the films to 54 minutes they were perfect for a 60-minute time slot with commercials.

In 1952, Boyd announced a brand new Hopalong Cassidy TV series. By this time he had amassed enough money to buy-out the investors. Hoppy was now all his!

That year, the Hopalong Cassidy television series went on the air for NBC. The first dozen episodes were actually re-edited 30-minute versions of his '46 through '48 film season. Boyd would supplement the heavily edited films with a voice-over merely explaining what had been going on.

After the first twelve shows the regular television series was filmed. While Andy Clyde continued in the role of California Carlson on the radio program, Boyd decided to hire Edgar Buchanan to play Red Connors on the TV show. Connors was a character right from Mulford's stories. He had appeared in some of the early films played by Frank McGlynn, Jr. Buchanan just wasn't funny and Boyd asked Clyde to join the series, but he refused out of pride for not being asked in the first place.

Another problem was that Boyd didn't hire a young sidekick to handle any romantic chores or fisticuffs. He probably figured that there wouldn't be enough time in a thirty-minute show for a third actor to share the spotlight. This caused the program to move at a snails pace, along with Boyd continuing to supply voice–over narration to move the story along, which it didn't. Hoppy was a much older character by this time, and Red wasn't much of a dashing figure either. The TV program would have benefited from a younger third lead, making it the traditional trio of the films. As it stands, the television show is more talk then action; death for a show that was primarily, by this point, aimed at children and adults who had grown up with the Hoppy films.

It's a pity about Clyde. He could have added the zest that the TV series desperately needed. As it stands, Hoppy and Red just look like a couple of old-timers trying to relive past glories; unlike the Lone Ranger, Gene Autry, Roy Rogers, and The Cisco Kid, whose TV shows still have moments of action and humor.

Boyd made one welcome concession to his fans. He permanently returned to his famous Hoppy costume, albeit a bit darker and streamlined.

As mentioned before, so popular was Hopalong Cassidy

that, as a favor to his old boss Cecil B. DeMille, Boyd appeared in costume in *The Greatest Show on Earth* (1952).

Appearing in a film for DeMille brought William Boyd full-circle. He had turned adversity on its ear and made it on his own terms. The Hopalong Cassidy film series holds up extremely well today, especially the Sherman films, and they are extremely enjoyable to watch.

Not bad for a washed up matinee idol whose star fell drastically due to mistaken identity. He would rise even higher due to his perseverance in the face of adversity. He could have given up and walked away from his career. Aren't we lucky that he didn't?

Silent film idol, William Boyd, from "The Last Frontier," 1926.

Western performer, Bill "Cowboy Rambler" Boyd, (2nd from left), appeared in six films for Producers Releasing Corporation, in 1942.

HOPALONG CASSIDY THROUGH THE YEARS

1935

1936

*Top left to right:
Hoppy in 1941; in 1943.
Center: Rand Brooks, Bill
Boyd, Andy Clyde, and
Elaine Riley in 1948
Bottom: Bill Boyd as he
looked during the 1950s*

CHAPTER SIX
THE SMILEY CONSPIRACY
—or—
KICKIN' BACK WITH THE SIDEKICKS

With people finding conspiracies under every rock these days here's another one to ponder. Did Herbert J. Yates and Republic Pictures set out to ruin Lester "Smiley" Burnette's film career, or did he do it on his own? Oh, it happened to be sure, but was it on purpose?

Anybody who knew Smiley would never have called him a shrewd businessman. Although he was a talented songwriter and musician he would sell his songs for peanuts, not caring about the importance of royalties until it was too late. While royalties would start filling the pockets of those who bought the songs Smiley would write, or co-write, he would see none of it.

Gene Autry and Lester "Smiley" Burnette had been performing together on the "National Barn Dance" radio program in Chicago, which was broadcast over WLS and carried by NBC, when Hollywood beckoned. Gene, an acute businessman, was smart enough to put Smiley under personal contract before they moved to California and the fame that Republic Pictures would bring them. Did he look at Smiley as a commodity or a friend? Maybe Gene looked on him as both.

Gene actually discovered Smiley when he was working at a small radio station in Tuscola, Illinois. Gene needed an accordion player and Smiley had been recommended to him as the best musician around. He signed Smiley for $35 a week.

Gene never made any bones about his relationship with

Smiley. Openly he always made Smiley look good. Gene, himself, would tell people that the song "Ridin' Down the Canyon" was written while he and Smiley were traveling through Arizona's beautiful Oak Creek Canyon on the way to Hollywood, and that he paid Smiley only five dollars for the song rights. *"Smiley was sitting in the back seat of the car and asked me if I wanted to buy a song. I said I didn't know because I hadn't heard it yet. "* Neither Gene nor Smiley could read music, so they waited until they could stop where somebody was able to play the song for them. Gene liked it and bought it from Smiley. Both their names would appear as co-writers on the song. What part did Gene have, if any, in helping to write the song? Possibly Gene helped refine it to fit his style.

Gene wasn't the only one to do this. Songwriting is a business, and the bigger you are the better your chances of people wanting to have your name attached to their product.

A case to support this is the story behind Gene's theme song "Back in the Saddle Again." Many film historians state that the song was introduced in Gene's 1939 film **Rovin' Tumbleweeds**, but this just isn't so! It was originally written and performed by Ray Whitley for the 1938 George O'Brien Western **Border G-Man**, where Whitley received sole authorship.

The story goes that in 1938, Whitley was awakened at 5:00 am by a call from RKO asking him for a new song for the O'Brien film. Returning to the bedroom he said to his wife, *"Well, I'm back in the saddle again."* She then said to him, *"You've got the title for the song right there."* He wrote a simple version of the song and performed it in the film. Gene heard the song and loved it. Gene offered

Whitley $350 for the song and he accepted the offer. The song now lists Gene and Ray Whitley as co-authors.

Although Whitley would appear alongside O' Brien and Tim Holt in a series of Westerns for RKO, plus a series of short features of his own, his lasting fame comes from being listed as the co-writer of "Back in the Saddle." Whitley would appear many times throughout the years with Gene and never complained openly about the deal, even though it made Gene Autry millions of dollars.

Smiley, on the other hand, didn't have the business acumen to deal with the likes of Gene Autry. Smiley would later complain that songs he had written were published under other people's names and that he was paid fifty dollars per song.

The royalty issue would become a bone of contention between Smiley and Gene in later years, but let's not forget that it was really Gene Autry who made Smiley a star to begin with. Gene was a shrewd businessman. Smiley wasn't.

Gene recognized the value of Smiley and that's why he put him under a personal contract. Gene also knew that he was the star and made sure that he was treated as such in each and every script. Smiley would have his moments to shine, however Gene would wisely make sure that the reigns were pulled in on him before his antics got out of hand. But they worked well together, there's no mistake about that! Gene made you believe that a cowpoke like himself would put up with the shenanigans of a clod like Frog Millhouse.

Later examples of Smiley's excesses can be seen in his films with Sunset Carson and Charles Starrett, where he was given more screen time. In those instances he could wear out his welcome, as would any comical sidekick with too much to do.

Smiley was the first and most popular sidekick in a regular western series. However, with time, Republic would find competition for Smiley in George Hayes, just like they did when they brought in Roy Rogers to hopefully keep Gene Autry in line. In Roy and Gene's case they moved about comfortably within their own realms. Gene was top dog and Roy took up the slack in case Gene decided to leave. When Gene left, to serve his country during World War II, Republic used all their resources and made Roy the top dog. The debate will always continue as to whether Gene or Roy is the real King of the Cowboys, but to the two stars it never really mattered.

Smiley, on the other hand, never had the power that Gene and Roy enjoyed. He could never carry a picture, although Republic Pictures tried that route when they paired him with Sunset Carson, but his clowning just seemed to get in the way of the action. George Hayes would eventually overtake Smiley in popularity because of Republic's mishandling of the rotund sidekick.

His fall from grace happened gradually. In my opinion Republic Pictures and its president, Herbert J. Yates, need to take some of the blame for the downfall. But did they do it on purpose? You decide as I give you the facts.

Smiley was the first official sidekick in a western series, there's no mistake about that. Before 1935 there were character actors in roles that might be deemed as sidekicks, but their characters and the names would change from film to film. George Hayes and Al St. John were two such actors.

Hayes would actually start with the Hopalong Cassidy

series one month before Smiley and Gene's first official starring vehicle, *Tumbling Tumbleweeds* (9/35), ever hit the screen. However, Hayes was cast as various characters in the first four "Hoppys," before permanently taking on the role of sidekick Windy Halliday. Therefore, Smiley's character of "Frog Millhouse" was the first continuing sidekick character.

At the time, there were two polls to judge a western star's popularity. The Boxoffice Poll was voted on by the movie going public, while the Motion Picture Herald Poll was voted on by exhibitors. Smiley would first appear in the Boxoffice Poll top ten of 1939 in the number nine spot. He would be the only sidekick to break the top ten until 1941, when George Hayes entered in the number ten spot of the Boxoffice Poll. This was after his move to Republic Pictures. By that time Smiley was on both polls, placing at number five in the Motion Picture Herald Poll and number six in the Boxoffice Poll.

George "Gabby" Hayes wouldn't make both polls until 1944. This was during the time of Smiley's downward slide from popularity. At that time, Smiley was at number three in the Motion Picture Herald Poll, while Gabby was number four. In the public opinion poll, the Boxoffice Poll, Smiley was number five while Gabby was clear down the list at number eight. It was a strange year, however, for even old-timer Hoot Gibson appeared at number nine!

The turning point was 1945, when Smiley came in at number five on the Motion Picture Herald Poll, while Gabby came in at number two, right after Roy Rogers his usual partner in the movies. The movie going public voted Gabby number four in popularity, right after Hoppy, in the Boxoffice Poll, while Smiley didn't even appear on

61

the list. In all fairness, for some reason only six names appear on that list in '45.

Today mainly fans of the western genre remember Smiley. Gabby, on the other hand, is often recognized, mimicked, and given credit as the sidekick that made being a second banana in Westerns popular. In the movie *Blazing Saddles* Mel Brooks lovingly presents a parody of all the ingredients that went into a B western, right down to the "Gabby" Johnson character played by film director Jack Starrett, but billed as Claude Ennis, Jr.

Smiley was definitely the more talented of the two, but Gabby's character was more versatile. How can you be the most talented and not the most versatile? The secret is in the character. Depth of character wasn't exactly a requirement in order to be a sidekick, but George Hayes created a character that could actually work on many different levels while Smiley didn't, or wasn't allowed to. To be fair, George Hayes had been honing his character on film for many years before Smiley ever came to Hollywood. But it's hard to ever take Smiley seriously; with the ridiculous clownish costume he usually wore, and his mugging, and broad antics. All this tends to negate any sense of drama. Watching his films with Gene, especially the Columbia films, and the few he did with Roy Rogers, you can see a hint of a more three dimensional character occasionally trying to break out, but the studio never allowed it to happen. They never allowed Smiley to grow and nurture his character in the A productions like they did George Hayes.

Smiley could probably run musical circles around the singing western heroes that appeared on the screen during the '30s through the early '50s. But he was pigeonholed as an oaf.

It's true that Gabby generally played a stereo-typical gruff old-timer, but his character's attitude and costume could adapt to the surroundings and feelings from picture to picture. Republic recognized the versatility of Gabby and used him in A films as well as B productions, his contract stipulated that he would appear in both. He might show up in a Roy Rogers oater with patches on his britches, a battered hat, and an overplayed sour disposition, but you knew he had a soft heart. He could then turn right around and support John Wayne in a major Republic Pictures release. He was essentially playing the same character with a subdued, more standard, attire befitting an A picture. He would then downplay his grumbling, ever so slightly, to denote the more serious attitude of the bigger production. The character was basically the same, but the attitude could change depending on the picture. He had many facets to his character's personality.

Smiley was a great musician, while Gabby was an actor, and a good actor was more valuable to a studio. A good sidekick actor could enhance a hero's performance; it was an asset. But a terrific musician, like Smiley, might threaten to steal the show from the hero, especially if he was a singing cowboy.

Gene could make sure that Smiley's contributions were limited, but there were also times when Gene would let Smiley shine, and those moments could be magic. There's no doubt that these two worked extremely well together. Even if Gene's name appeared above the title, and Smiley's didn't, people associated the two. This became a problem for Gene. It would become evident, as time went on, that Gene had protected Smiley from the vultures at Republic Pictures, even while using the musician/comedian for his own benefit. But then again, I can't stress enough that there more than likely would have been no Smiley "Frog Millhouse" Burnette without Gene Autry.

Smiley's downfall can be attributed to three important events: 1) Republic Pictures hiring George Hayes, 2) the departure of Gene Autry in 1942, and, most importantly 3) Republic Pictures mishandling his career by partnering him with inadequate stars.

To put it all into perspective, let's start at the beginning of Smiley's career in Hollywood.

Did Gene have to take Smiley with him to Hollywood? Absolutely not, Gene obviously saw that Smiley would be an asset. Gene placed Smiley under a personal contact, even going to Smiley's home and promising his parents that he would personally take care of him in that jungle known as Hollywood.

Gene took another asset with him, steel guitar player Frankie Marvin. Marvin was eventually relegated to the background; his true talents would be displayed behind the scenes as a respected musician and songwriter, along with his brother Johnny.

Did Gene write the songs with Smiley? Like other stars Gene would buy songs outright from Smiley, possibly refining them to fit his style; there's nothing wrong there. However, this was definitely a bad business practice on Smiley's part and it would come back to haunt him.

Smiley seemed to live for the moment, while Gene had an eye on the future. A quick buck was Smiley's goal, while Gene had his mind on the whole game. A fortune is founded on risk, and Smiley didn't seem to be willing to take the chance. While Gene was building an empire, Smiley was using his money for self-serving purposes like building a recording studio in his home.

And yet at other times Smiley could be extremely frugal. Once, after shooting a scene where he was pelted with tomatoes, he gathered up the spent tomatoes, took them back to his trailer, and made a tomato soup from them.

In the beginning Smiley may have been a crutch for Gene. A sounding board Gene may have felt he needed. They worked well together on the "National Barn Dance," so Gene probably felt that the teaming could be the magic that would put him over in Hollywood. As time went on, Smiley began to feel that Gene was taking advantage of him. Gene, on the other hand, may have felt that Smiley was taking advantage as well.

Oliver Drake, who produced, directed and wrote a number of Westerns, knew the duo quite well. *"I was writing some of the stories and music for the films, and we were pals when Gene first started. Gene'd say, 'What do you think about it?' I'd say, 'Well, it's a good script and Smiley doesn't have too much to do.'"* Obviously Gene was concerned about the extent of Smiley's antics in his films. Gene's worries were justified; something Republic Pictures would learn on their own when they let Smiley run wild.

Roy Rogers worked differently with Smiley. His character was more flamboyant than Gene's. He could easily work within the framework of Smiley's routines, with ease and style, and incorporate them into the action.

Both Gene and Smiley would collect "clingers-on." People whose prime goal is to maintain a fringe position in show business by leeching off the talented and successful. Smiley's people would tell him that he didn't need Gene and Gene's would let him know if Smiley was getting out of hand. As Drake tells it: *"They kept trying and trying to breakup Smiley Burnette and Autry. They'd tell Gene, 'Smiley Burnette has too much to do in this picture.'"*

Jimmy Wakely, a singing star in his own right puts much of the blame on the film distributors. *"The distributors kept saying to Smiley that Gene couldn't make it without him, and they were wrong."*

Indeed they were wrong. As Gene grew more confident with himself on screen, Smiley may have become an albatross around his neck; considered a duo by many this may have rankled Gene. But as he would say in retrospect about his partnership with Smiley: *"In that part of the Southwest, where I was born, they had a saying to describe a man who was loyal: 'He'll do to ride the river.'"* Gene and Smiley were a great duo, the best example of the hero/sidekick combination. They would always be friends and companions in their films together. Smiley would generally act upon a situation with some piece of comic business and Gene would react to his tomfoolery, sometimes even taking part in the situation, which was always a joy to watch. As time went on, Gene became more comfortable with this format.

Roy and Gabby never really fit the hero/sidekick role like Gene and Smiley. Usually they would meet during the course of the story, with Gabby being the reactor in his relationship with the hero. He would react and respond to events around him with a crotchety attitude, but ready to fight alongside the hero when he needed to. Roy and Gabby would have a deep affection for each other that was more like a father and son. Nobody ever questioned why an intelligent hero like Roy would depend on someone like the elder sidekick, but you might wonder why someone like Gene Autry might put his faith in someone like Frog Millhouse.

None-the-less, Gene and Smiley must be considered the penultimate team, but the feeling of shared warmth was very rarely there like it was with Roy and Gabby. Companionship? Yes. Warmth. No. George Hayes had the same type of relationship with Hopalong Cassidy, which was hard to replace when he left for Republic Pictures. It's reported that Hayes found it hard to work with Boyd, but this never came across on screen. Harry "Pop" Sherman finally found his replacement in Andy Clyde.

Gene would eventually find a more comfortable sidekick in the less threatening Pat Buttram. But you have to wonder how Gene would have fared with Gabby by his side for a film or two? They actually did appear together in the larger budgeted *Melody Ranch* in 1940, but this film also featured Jimmy Durante, and can't really be considered a regular Gene Autry vehicle in the strictest sense.

As the B Westerns gained a set pattern, the studios would divide their stars and sidekicks into two different types of duos. They would either start the picture as true blue friends and saddle pals, or the hero would ride into town and meet the sidekick during the course of the story, possibly already knowing each other from some past experience.

From Gene and Smiley's first starring feature, *Tumbling Tumbleweeds* (9/35) thru *The Old Barn Dance* (1/38), they did twenty-one features, plus Maynard's two efforts and *The Phantom Empire* serial. Then Gene walked.

Outwardly, Gene said he left because Herbert J. Yates, the president of Republic Pictures, was forcing theater owners to "block buy" his films. The act of block buying forced theater owners to buy films they normally wouldn't show in order to get one or two that they wanted.

Gene found out that Yates was forcing theater owners to buy the rights to films they couldn't use in order to get the Autry films, which were in great demand. As the story goes, Gene walked out on his contract saying he would return when the practice of block buying was discontinued. He would be gone for almost eight months. By midsummer of '38, an understanding was reached between Yates and Gene. Did the practice of block-buying stop? Nope! But Gene got a substantial raise, which is what he was after all along. Gene had been receiving $100 per week for his work. By 1938 it had jumped to $350 per week. When Gene returned his salary went up substantially. His new deal would call for him to make $6,000 per film for his first two productions and then escalate to $10,000 per film after that; this was to continue through 1939.

Smiley, by this time, was gaining in popularity as well. By April of '38, he was playing sidekick to Republic's newest acquisition, Roy Rogers. *Under Western Stars* was originally to be an Autry vehicle titled *Washington Cowboy*, but when Gene walked out on his contract it was retooled for Roy. The second film Smiley did with Roy, *Billy the Kid Returns*, was shot right after *Under Western Stars*, but it wouldn't be released until Autry had returned to the fold and had two films produced and released with Smiley. These were *Gold Mine in the Sky* (7/38) and *Man from Music Mountain* (8/38).

Clearly, Autry was back in the saddle and Roy, for the moment, was relegated to the number two spot. It makes sense that Yates would hold up the release of *Billy the Kid*

Returns until Gene had two new pictures out for Republic. Keep in mind that for the first two pictures Gene would receive $12,000! This alone was cause enough for Yates to want to rush the Autry vehicles through production, make Gene happy, and forestall any Roger's product for a few months. It would also let everyone know that Gene was numero uno at the studio. But there was a more important reason for Yates to quickly get Autry product out there in quick order. Distributors and theater owners were complaining that there hadn't been any new Autry films in 6 months. This was the main reason that Yates would come to terms with Gene Autry and get two more films out there as soon as possible. Several months would lapse between Roy's first and second release for Republic Pictures, due to the fact that Yates felt pressured to get Gene Autry back in the saddle.

Gene had proven that he was the top dog. His budgets were enlarged, but larger doesn't always mean better. Republic began to add splashy musical numbers to his films, while Roy's became lean action fests. The musical element in the Autry films probably appealed to Smiley. When Autry left for World War II, the larger budgets and splashy musical numbers would be assigned to Roy's films.

After Gene's return in '38 things couldn't have been better for Smiley. By 1939 Smiley was in the Boxoffice Poll top ten, between Tex Ritter and Bob Livingston, the only sidekick to appear in this prestigious group. But within two years things would begin to change.

In late 1938 Republic Pictures producer Sol Seigel signed George Hayes away from Harry "Pop" Sherman, producer of the Hopalong Cassidy series. Seigel felt that Hayes would be an asset in Republic's B pictures, as well as the A product with the likes of John Wayne and Richard Dix. It was soon discovered that Hayes had a photographic memory and could learn his lines after simply reading through the script. Producers would expand his parts after learning this fact.

Hayes would be kept quite busy in the different categories of films that Herbert Yates had devised for his studio. Yates divided his films into four categories. The "Jubilee" films were the cheapest, shot in seven days for a budget of around $50,000. The "Anniversary" films were usually shot in fourteen days for around $200,000. The "Deluxe" films were shot in twenty-two days and budgeted at around $500,000, and finally the "Premiere" films. This final category was created by Yates to entice directors like John Ford. The schedule on these pictures would be around a month for about $1,000,000.

But Smiley never seemed to be in the running for any of the larger budgeted films. He would make a few B films and serials for Mascot and Republic away from the Autry vehicles; even a film at 20th Century Fox, **Border Patrol** (1936) with George O' Brien, but that would be about the extent of it.

It would appear that Yates might have respected George Hayes and his talent, while he utilized Smiley as a popular sidekick in the lower echelon pictures. Hayes had been a respected character actor for years, while Smiley Burnette was, more or less, created by Republic Pictures.

Before you could say, *"Yur dern tootin,"* Gabby was riding alongside Roy for Republic Pictures while Sherman was still releasing his Hopalong Cassidy films through Paramount Pictures. George, or "Gabby Whitaker," the name Hayes would mostly use in his films after his move to Republic, even added some support to Smiley and Gene in the film *In Old Monterey* (8/39).

A real slap in the face came in 1940 when Republic cast Gene, without Smiley, in the big budget musical extravaganza, **Melody Ranch**. Gene would star alongside heavyweights Jimmy Durante and Ann Miller. And guess who else appeared in the film? None other than...George "Gabby" Hayes! Considering Smiley was a real musical genius, his omission in this A musical must have been a real sore spot. It's unthinkable to not have Smiley in a film such as this. The chance to see Smiley in a large budget musical alongside Durante and Miller would have been a real highlight in the canon of Autry/Burnette films.

But it would get worse when later that very same year Smiley would be slighted once more! Gene appeared without him once again in the 20th Century Fox film *Shooting High*. Gene took second billing to the juvenile star Jane Withers.

Withers, a second string Shirley Temple for Fox, was very talented but lacked the looks it took to give little Shirley much competition. As she got older her career would begin to lag until she gained fame once again in the '60s and 70s as "Josephine the Plumber" in the Comet Cleanser commercials.

Shooting High would be Gene's only foray outside his contracted studio, Republic or Columbia. It was also the last time he played a character other than Gene Autry. His character's name in this effort was "Will Carson."

During this time, Gabby, besides riding with Roy, could be seen in A pictures for Republic like **Man of Conquest** (1939) with Richard Dix, and **The Dark Command** (1940) with the strong cast of John Wayne, Walter Pidgeon, Claire

Trevor and Roy Rogers. It would be Roy's only A production at his home studio.

It's also a real pleasure to see the true fondness that Roy and Gabby share in their films. It seems to be there from the very start. In their second film together, *In Old Caliente* (6/39), Roy and Gabby have a terrific duet, "We're Not Coming Out to Dance Tonight." It makes you wish that there had been more of these numbers in their films together.

The beginning of the end for Smiley, as number one sidekick, really began when Gene left to serve his country. After finishing **Bells of Capistrano** (9/42) Gene left Republic for World War II.

It's interesting to note that Gene came back the same year Smiley moved to Columbia Pictures. Gene's leaving to serve his country would allow him to start anew upon his return, and without Smiley Burnette; although Gene couldn't have known that Smiley would leave Republic Pictures before his return.

When Gene did returned, Smiley was already riding with Charles Starrett AKA The Durango Kid. It was assumed that Gene would return to Republic Pictures and resume his career there, but he had other ideas. The reason Gene Autry did the handful of films at Republic when he returned to Hollywood will be explained later.

After Gene's departure for active duty, Smiley was given a plump position. By December of 1942, Smiley was sharing screen time with Gabby and Roy in **Hearts of the Golden West**. After that one, Gabby left the series to become sidekick for another popular Republic star, Bill Elliott. Meanwhile, Smiley rode his horse, Ring-eyed Nellie or Nelly, Ring-eye, Black-eyed Nellie or plain Nelly take your pick. along-side Roy and Trigger for three more films. Smiley complimented Roy very nicely, and actually gave him a true sidekick in the strictest sense. Roy was too strong a personality for Smiley to ever overpower and he always seemed to enjoy the jokes.

During Gabby's time with Elliott he made the Boxoffice Poll for the first time, in 1941 at number ten. Smiley weighed in – no pun intended – at number six on the Boxoffice Poll and number five on the exhibitors Motion Picture Herald Poll; still a strong standing for the side-kick. Hayes would continue to appear in A Pictures during this time as well.

But Republic, in their infinite wisdom, decided to create a new "prefab" hero out of whole cloth for Smiley to ride with. The studio was already in the lead of western programmer films, with the biggest cowboy stars, so it didn't really make sense when the studio tapped Eddie Dew, a supporting player in Westerns, for the role of new hero "John Paul Revere." Smiley was assigned as his sidekick. Herbert J. Yates and Republic may have felt that Smiley, being a top ten sidekick, would be able to add strength to the series to make it a winner.

With powerful stars like Roy Rogers, Bill Elliott, Don "Red" Barry, Allan Lane (before he added the "Rocky"), and the still popular Three Mesquiteers, it was a losing battle. Robert Livingston replaced Dew after two films. Livingston completed three more with Smiley and then the series was discontinued. It was during this series that the films were listed as "A Smiley Burnette Production." The studio was obviously trying to make Smiley into a power to be reckoned with, but it would all backfire very shortly.

During the time Smiley was moving about in the company of lesser stars, Gabby was appearing in A films like *War of the Wildcats* and *Tall in the Saddle* with John Wayne. He was also continuing a successful run as Bill Elliott's sidekick. Next to Roy Rogers and John Wayne, Elliott would prove to be Republic Pictures largest asset during the war years and Gabby was appearing with all three!

Meanwhile, Republic's most popular sidekick was given...Sunset Carson. Today we can scratch our heads and wonder what Republic Pictures was thinking when they hired Carson to star in a series of Westerns. "Likable" is the best thing that can be said about this honest to goodness cowboy. Carson claimed the title of "Champion Cowboy of South America," whatever that is, and was indeed born to the saddle. But an honest to goodness cowpoke doesn't necessarily make a good western star.

He had already appeared in *Stage Door Canteen* (1943) under the name Michael Harrison. The way he received his western film moniker is worth repeating. *"Republic thought my name was too long so they came up with the name Carson, and then they started kicking around several combinations. They came up with 'Cody' Carson, names like that. Yates looked out the window and saw a used car lot with a sign that read 'Sunset Motors,' and so he named me after a used car lot. It's a good thing he didn't name me 'Motors' Carson.*

With the exit of the extremely popular Don "Red" Barry and the demise of the John Paul Revere series, Yates hired Harrison. But would the fact that he couldn't act, or even read a line with any believability, get in the way? Guess not! His first movie for Republic was *Call Of the Rockies*

(7/44), where for the first and last time he was billed as Sonny "Sunset" Carson.

Peggy Stewart, who appeared in eight films with Sunset, loved working with him. *"I adored him, but he did have a hard time with lines. I would have to stand next to the camera and feed his lines to him, one at a time. He would then repeat, what we called "parrot," them back for the camera. He would drive the director crazy because he'd sometimes have to do up to six takes on a scene, and in a B Western that wasn't done."* Peggy has some wonderful stories about working with Sunset and how he would constantly mispronounce words in the script, or fail to pause for emphasis on certain lines. *"Sunset would tend to bunch all his lines together without any pauses. I'd wait until he was done and then I would say, 'Alright, is it my turn now?' I finally told him to go home and practice counting up to five between the lines that needed emphasizing. So the next day he came to work and we began shooting a scene. When it came time for Sunset to deliver his lines, he indeed would pause, but you could see his lips move as he counted the numbers!"* All in all, Peggy found Sunset Carson to be a joy to work with and she misses him dearly.

On the other hand, she doesn't have very nice things to say about Smiley Burnette. *"I didn't like him. He was so mean to Sunset. He would stand behind the camera and make fun of him. Smiley knew how to play to the camera and Sunset didn't. So Smiley would make sure that he was in Sunset's key-light, which would cause shadows on Sunset. He would also try to stand between Sunset and the camera and try to up-stage him with pieces of business that would distract from Sunset during his scenes. The director would constantly get after Smiley for that and I'd*

75

try to make sure that he didn't get away with it either!"

In one of Sunset's final interviews he too talked about his relationship with Smiley. *"Gabby Hayes was the measuring stick with which to judge all other sidekicks. He was a real gentleman. Smiley was kinda cold for our first couple of films. I don't know if he was told to or not, but he kinda softened up around the last picture."*

To be fair, June Storey, who worked with Smiley, would relate how he would take a pan of cool water, after a day of filming, and wash and massage her feet. It just shows that there is good and bad in us all.

Sunset would never make the Boxoffice Poll, but he would appear in 1946 on the Motion Picture Herald Poll at number eight. Today, he's remembered more for his colorful name rather than his western series. However I do have to admit I have a soft spot for his films.

Around this period Smiley received a new contract where he would make $1,000 per day! It was obvious that the studio wanted to make him happy. I'm sure you would have to agree that, even today, an amount such as that would be nice to earn per day. The only problem is that it would only last as long as he was working on a film, and his films were made in about seven days. Still, in 1944 alone he made four movies, so that ain't hay for the 1940s!

Another precedent was set with the Sunset Carson series. Smiley was given top billing over the hero. Republic still must have had faith in Smiley's audience appeal, even after the dismal showing of the John Paul Revere series. But it could also be said that they were using Smiley to try and further the careers of their so-called up and coming cowboy stars. They tried it with Eddie Dew and it didn't work. Now they were using Smiley's good name to try and create a star out of Carson. It would be to the detriment of Smiley's career. Still, all in all, giving Smiley his own "Smiley Burnette Productions," star billing over the hero, and a whopping $1,000 per day, the studio must have believed the rotund Mr. Burnette could do it. But while Smiley labored in what might be termed experimental projects, Gabby was creeping in through the back door to become the leading sidekick, by lending firm support in quality A and B films with top stars.

With Gene no longer around to look after Smiley, he was at Herbert J. Yates' mercy. While Gabby was finishing his stint with Wild Bill Elliott, and re-joining Roy Rogers for another series of fourteen films, Smiley's unquestionable talents were being wasted. With his four Sunset Carson films completed, he left Republic Pictures for good in December of 1944. Republic probably felt that they weren't getting their money's worth anymore, and besides, they now had George "Gabby" Hayes to promote.

In '44 Smiley was ranked in the Boxoffice Poll in fifth place, with Gabby in the number eight spot. The Motion Picture Herald Poll had them ranked number three and number four respectively. As I stated before, by 1945 the roles had reversed. It was evident that Gabby now reigned supreme as Republic Pictures top sidekick.

With the signing of George Hayes, the departure of Gene Autry, and the mishandling of Lester "Smiley" Burnette by Republic Pictures, it's hard to believe that the worst insult was yet to come; and from none other than Gene Autry. But before that was to come, Smiley would begin his second most prolific run as sidekick to the most popular western hero at Columbia Pictures, "The Durango Kid."

Smiley's last film for Republic was released in December of 1944. He wouldn't have a new movie released until February of 1946. This may have hurt his standing in the polls, but when he did hook up with a new western hero he hooked up with a real winner!

Now known as simply Smiley Burnette in his films, although his first film with Starrett called him "Smiley Butterbean," due to Republic retaining the rights to "Frog Millhouse," he was signed by Columbia Pictures to play sidekick opposite Charles Starrett in his popular Durango Kid series.

Starrett had been a popular staple on the western movie circuit since 1935. In 1945 Starrett revived a character he had played in a 1940 film called *The Durango Kid*. The new film, appropriately titled *The Return of the Durango Kid*, was a hit. Thereafter, Starrett played the character exclusively.

Dub "Cannonball" Taylor had been Starrett's sidekick since 1943, but after seven in the Durango Kid series he was replaced by Smiley. Columbia, probably wanting to capitalize on Smiley's still popular name and face value, cast him in the series. Some believe that, with the signing of Smiley, the series started to slip down hill. Starrett and Taylor had an easy-going quality to their relationship, with Taylor not being too obtrusive, and a terrific musician to boot. Smiley became more of a co-star to Starrett with, at times, caustic and shoddy results.

Later on, during his time at the western festivals, Starrett was frank about his relationship with Smiley. *"Smiley and I didn't hit it off too good at first. He told me he had come over to Columbia to give my series a shot in the arm. That remark did not set too well with me."* It sounds like Smiley may have had a bit of an ego problem. Keep in mind that he hadn't been under contract to any studio for over a year.

Once again, leave it to Jimmy Wakely to put things into perspective. *"Smiley wasn't very good with Bob Livingston, Sunset Carson and Eddie Dew so Republic let him go."* To be fair, it's hard to be good with inferior product, but, if Republic let him go, Smiley is lucky that he ended up at Columbia instead of Monogram or PRC.

One more example of Smiley's ego occurred when "Arkansas" Slim Andrews appeared in an Autry western with Smiley. *"I had a good scene with Smiley,"* as Andrews would tell it. *"I thought it turned out pretty funny, but when it was over Smiley said, 'Hey Bud, you're funny, but you won't be in any more of Autry's pictures; I'm the comedian around here.' Smiley knew what he was talking about and I never made anymore movies with Autry."*

The Starrett productions didn't improve with Smiley, rather they seemed to begin a downward slide toward tackiness. It's been hinted that, due to the salary that was afforded Smiley, costs were cut elsewhere. Sets and action seemed restricted. In some cases, past entries in the series were recycled with a minimum of new footage, so they could qualify as a new feature. To be fair, the programmer Westerns were slowly becoming out dated and Columbia wasn't making their bread and butter with these films like Republic was.

Smiley should have added the needed zest to smooth over budget cuts, but it doesn't work and his routines seem long and overworked. He also appears to be in neutral during many of his appearances, simply going through the motions as if uninterested in the proceedings. As time would move on, his thick dark hair would give way to a more mature distinguished peppery white. The mature look, although distinguished looking, doesn't quite fit with the foolish antics of Smiley's character.

One of the films in the series, which used an exorbitant amount of old footage, was **Streets of Ghost Town** (8/50). Over one half of the film was old footage. It featured a young actress who would make her name in western movies playing opposite Rex Allen in several of his films. Her name is Mary Ellen Kay. Today Ellen is as pretty and youthful as ever. A close friend of mine, she shared her recollections of Smiley with me. *"I remember Smiley as being extremely friendly and helpful. He was always playful on the set and was constantly making me laugh. I enjoyed working with him, especially since I grew up watching he and Gene in the movies."*

Although Smiley appears tired and uninterested in many of these films, it would seem that he had found a home where he could be somewhat happy. Smiley was given a fair amount to do, much of the time to the detriment to the series. His comical interludes could stop the action and damage the momentum that had been built to that point. These routines may or may not have anything to do with the plot, but they became more and more ridiculous.

Smiley would appear as Starrett's sidekick through fifty-seven films, just one less than he did with Autry, discounting serials and Maynard's film.

Smiley Burnette's best years had been with Gene Autry despite their differences. Audiences would have loved to have the "Dymanic Duo of Westerns" back together again. Many assumed it would happen upon Gene's return after the war. But it wasn't to be.

Gene's return to Republic Pictures wasn't exactly to his liking. He wanted to make a clean break and start anew. Approaching Columbia Pictures he made a deal for his own production company. It was then that Herbert Yates reared his presidential head. Yates insisted that Gene Autry owed Republic Pictures a series of films. Yates maintained that Gene had signed a seven-year contract with the studio before leaving and that it was put on hold while Autry served his country. The star felt that the contract had simply lapsed during his time away from the studio. After going to court over the issue, Gene agreed to do five more films for Republic Pictures.

The choice for his sidekick was a curious one. Comic actor Sterling Holloway was chosen, but it was a most insipid piece of casting. Holloway was ineffective in the role and totally out of his league, much like burlesque comic Pinky Lee would be when Republic cast him as Roy Roger's sidekick in 1951.

Holloway didn't think much of the results either: *"I didn't care for my role as Autry's sidekick, and I really didn't care for horses. Horses and I had a mutual agreement, they hated me and I hated them. I was glad when the Autry pictures were over and I could get back to roles for which I was more suited."*

Mercifully Holloway never appeared as a sidekick in any other Westerns. He gained his greatest fame as the voice of Winnie the Pooh for Disney.

It's interesting to note that both Gene and Roy were given ineffectual sidekicks – Holloway and Lee respectively – for their last set of films at Republic Pictures. Could Yates have been punishing them for wanting to leave his studio?

Besides the quality of sidekick he was given, Gene was dissatisfied with the new stories that were handed to him. Herbert Yates wanted the old Autry back, but Gene couldn't give it to him. The war had taken its toll on Gene and the viewing public. People weren't interested in splashy music fests incorporated into their Westerns and Gene wasn't interested in doing that type of film. Even Roy would tone down the big numbers, going more for relevant human-interest stories and stressing more action.

Yates would also repeat the same action he took when Autry left in 1937 and he signed Roy Rogers to a contract. Republic Pictures would sign Monte Hale as their next singing cowboy in 1946. The move wasn't as successful as expected. Yates would gain a full-fledged singing cowboy when he signed Rex Allen in 1949. He would make his first starring western, *The Arizona Cowboy*, in 1949. The following year Monte Hale made his last film for Republic, appropriately titled, *The Vanishing Westerner*.

By the time Republic's five films were completed and released Gene was firmly entrenched at Columbia Pictures. He would make a deal with the studio wherein he would have his own production unit. He now would be able to make the kind of films he wanted to make. Gene would play down the musical interludes and introduce a more somber tone. If a bad guy needed killing he was killed, no bones about it! They were Autry films, make no mistake, but Gene Autry had matured and so did his films.

With Smiley at Columbia, and now Gene at the same studio, it would seem that the scene was set for a film reunion. It didn't happen, at least not yet.

When Autry left Republic, he took many of the filmmakers from that studio with him. His producer Armand

Schaefer, directors John Butler and Frank McDonald, writers John K. Butler and Jack Townley, and Photographer William Bradford all joined Gene Autry at his new studio. It was like old home week. The only one, it seems, who wasn't invited to join the reunion was Smiley Burnette.

Initially Gene didn't even have a sidekick. He finally settled on a comedian who had appeared in his second Columbia film, *The Strawberry Roan* (8/48). His name was Pat Buttram. Like Gene and Smiley, Pat Buttram had come from the *National Barn Dance*, broadcast over WLS in Chicago, where Gene had known him previously.

Gene and Pat became life long friends. They would not only do films together, but Gene's *Melody Ranch* radio program and television show as well. Pat Buttram not only provided slapstick, but a verbal cornpone type of humor that lent itself well to the medium of radio and programmer Westerns. Although Buttram could join in on a musical number, he was never a threat to Gene. He was the perfect foil for the new image Gene was trying to convey. Pat was well aware of who his savior was in film, radio and television and never forgot it. As Gene would later say, *"If I was on stage and Pat was sitting behind me, if I needed a good joke he would hand one up to me."* It's obvious that Pat was perfectly happy to make Gene look good, which was just fine with Gene Autry.

As Pat Buttram would tell it: *"Smiley Burnette would rarely work radio; it wasn't his medium, so I did radio with Gene. When Gene was in the service, Smiley went with Charlie Starrett. When Gene came out of the Army in '46, he didn't have a sidekick in pictures, so he just put me in the pictures."*

This, of course, is revisionist history. Smiley didn't join

Starrett for four years after Gene left for the Army. Much of that time was spent toiling away in generally inferior productions, aside from those with Roy Rogers. It wasn't until 1946 that Smiley signed with Columbia Pictures and became Starrett's sidekick. Furthermore, when Gene did return to Republic Pictures, in 1946, he was paired with Sterling Holloway as his so-called sidekick for five films. These were released the later part of '46 through mid-1947. Gene's first film for Columbia was released in November of 1947. It wasn't until November of 1949 that Buttram actually teamed on the silver screen with the singing cowboy, although he had appeared in *The Strawberry Roan* in 1948. So basically Buttram overlooks the four years of Smiley's career following Gene's leaving for the service. In ignoring all this he moves himself up as Gene Autry's film sidekick by three years, from November of '49 to November of '46. Minor point? Maybe. Big discrepancy? You bet!

I also can't imagine Smiley not wanting to do radio appearances. Being a musician, and considering his background in radio, it's hard to believe Smiley would have balked at radio appearances. If Gene said he was going to do radio, Smiley would probably have done it too. Smiley may have been in an argument over royalties or some such thing, but who knows? So, with no proof to the contrary, I'll take Pat Buttram's word on this.

Another difference is in the way Buttram says he was treated during his time as Gene's sidekick. *"If the sidekick happened to get a little ahead of the star on his horse, the star would stop the scene and say, 'You get back; I want to be six feet ahead.' This was often the rule a lot of them had, but Autry wasn't that way at all."*

Buttram would occasionally talk quite candidly about Gene Autry's business acumen, like this humorous story: *"I remember Gene used to sell a Gene Autry songbook over the radio for 50 cents. Then he'd come in on Saturday and pick up his mail. He'd sit in front of the wastebasket, shake each envelope so the coins would slide down to one corner, and then hit it on the rim of the wastebasket. The envelope would break open, the money would fall out and he'd hand the envelope to his secretary. I'll always remember that wastebasket half full with silver."*

Pat Buttram had an extremely long career in acting and stand-up comedy. He obviously didn't cause Gene any grief, and he was rewarded for it. By the time Pat became Gene's sidekick, Autry was well into other endeavors that interested him far more then being a movie star. Autry was probably more comfortable and self-assured. He felt at ease with Buttram, a sidekick who didn't ask much, but gave 100%.

During Pat Buttram's tenure with Gene, fate took a hand and reunited Autry and Burnette. While filming Gene's television program in 1951, Pat almost had a foot severed doing a scene involving an exploding cannon. Gene asked Smiley to do his next film, **Whirlwind** (4/51), with him while Buttram mended. It was their first film together in almost ten years. It was also a one shot gig. The result was very satisfying. Smiley and Gene fit like a glove, and the more mature Smiley fit well into the proceedings. He gave a good accounting for him-self with not a lot of extra balderdash thrown in. He was given a good part and used it wisely. Just to see Gene and Smiley sing, with ease and comfort, the duet, "Tweedle O' Twill," was worth the price of admission. It was a terrific outing and the two fit in together better than ever! With the more somber tone Smiley tempered his character and brought home the bacon. A follow-up should have happened, but it was not to be.

Smiley finished this production between *Fort Savage Raiders* and *Snake River Desperadoes* with Charles Starrett. Starrett was an easygoing kind of guy and, unlike Gene Autry, he let Smiley do his thing with no restrictions. Like most comics, Smiley needed to be told when enough was enough. Gene could do that, but Starrett wouldn't. He would later admit that the series lost something when Dub Taylor was replaced by Smiley.

A couple of other issues began to fester within Smiley. In the early '50s, studios like Republic and stars like William Boyd were beginning to sell their old movies to television. Gene, who purchased the rights to all his films from Republic and owned his Columbia releases, refused to sell any of them to television. He knew they would be worth a lot more later on. He was also beginning a new television program, which was a good publicity tool for his new films still being released in the theaters. Each week, at the end of his television show, the announcer would remind you to be sure and see "Gene Autry and Champion in their latest feature length motion picture at a theater near you." A half hour show each week was one thing, but releasing your old films to television would create a glut of product. Gene felt that if someone could see your films on television they might not pay money to see you in a "theater near you." In a way you would be creating competition for yourself. It was all right for William Boyd to sell his films to the new medium, because he wasn't making any new films, and by that time television was his primary medium. But Gene was still making movies.

Another dispute cropped up over music royalties. Royalties to songs those years before Smiley had sold Gene the rights to. To be fair to Gene, Smiley had sold the rights to an enormous number of his songs to many different artists, and, in Smiley's own admission, for fifty dollars per song. Whoever bought and registered these songs would be the person indicated as the author and, as such, they would be entitled to all the royalties.

Obviously, Smiley was a terrible businessman and, by the late '40s, he was in financial trouble. The Durango Kid took his last ride in August of '52 and Smiley was without a series for the first time since late 1944. Smiley approached Gene about the songs they had "collaborated" on, and asked for some of the royalties. Gene, being the businessman that he was, refused. He did however offer his former sidekick a solution. Autry was preparing to produce his last six films for Columbia. He invited Smiley to do them with him. Smiley agreed.

Publicly Autry would later say, *"We had gone in together and we would go out together. Fair is fair."* Smiley would have probably thought it would be fair to split the royalties, but he needed the money the films would give him. In reality, Gene probably saw the pairing as a good publicity ploy for his final six films. Gene and Smiley, together again, would probably mean good box-office in the waning days of the programmer Westerns. Starting with *Winning of the West*, released in January of 1953, Smiley would lend support to Gene through *On Top of Old Smokey*, *Goldtown Ghost Raiders*, *Pack Train*, *Saginaw Trail*, and *Last of the Pony Riders*, all released between March and November of '53.

Smiley finished out his Columbia contract with Gene, while Pat Buttram continued his sidekick duties on Gene's TV and radio shows, as well as personal appearances.

After his film career ended Smiley went on the road. In 1963, he finally made it to the small screen in a regular role. As railroad engineer Charlie Pratt he appeared alongside former Mesquiteer Rufe Davis on the popular CBS television show *Petticoat Junction*. He was barely recognizable with his now white hair and lethargic attitude, but it was still good to see him once again. The series, produced by the same team responsible for *The Beverly Hillbillies*, was a hit and he continued on the series until his death on February 16, 1967.

Consequently, he would still continue to be haunted by Pat Buttram. The same production team came up with another hit rural show, *Green Acres*, and gave Buttram the plum part of Mr. Haney. The role fit Buttram like a glove, giving him the role of a lifetime. People who heretofore had never seen Buttram were tuning in to watch the antics of Mr. Haney and Arnold the pig every week.

In 1987 through 1988, Gene Autry and Pat Buttram hosted a weekly program for The Nashville Network called *Melody Ranch Theater*, which featured Gene's films. Gene would recall his days with Smiley Burnette fondly, and relate many complementary stories about the most talented sidekick of all.

Today, Smiley Burnette isn't remembered as well as his counterpart Gabby Hayes. It's a shame, for he was the sidekick who was there first and set the pace. He was the most talented of all the sidekicks, but his versatility was exploited and abused by others as well as his self. It possibly trapped him in a stereotypical mold in which nobody would let him escape. The curmudgeon character of Gabby Hayes allowed more leeway, more room to allow the hero to breath. Smiley was a powerhouse that could possibly overpower the hero if he were allowed to.

In the end, Smiley probably only had himself to blame for being so darn talented and yet so gullible.

Ironically, Smiley gave an up and coming western music star some sound advice concerning a possible future in films. Rex Allen was debating whether he should make the move from radio to the big screen. He complained to Smiley that he was making more money in radio then he would make working for Republic Pictures. Smiley told Allen that he should take the pay cut because he'll become a larger star in films and therefore sale more records, there-by making more money. Rex Allen took his advice and found it to be true. If Smiley had taken his own advice, rather then selling the rights to his musical product, he would have had no problems with money later in his life.

Rex would later make the comment to Smiley that he believed Gene Autry was so frugal that he probably still had the first dollar that he ever made. Smiley told Rex that he was wrong. *"He used his first dollar to buy a wallet."* He was probably a bit bitter in acknowledging the fact that Gene was a tight-fisted businessman.

Was there any conspiracy to ruin Smiley? Probably not consciously on anyone's part. Some of the blame has to be laid at the feet of the most talented sidekick to ever ride the range, Smiley himself. However, after all is said and done we should just enjoy what he's left us. When we think about sidekicks like, Cliff "Ukulele Ike" Edwards, Dub "Cannonball" Taylor, Rufe Davis, "Arkansas" Slim

Andrews, and yes, even Pat Buttram, remember, Lester "Smiley" Burnette was there first to pave the way.

Cliff "Ukulele Ike" Edwards

"Arkansas" Slim Andrews

"Dub" Taylor

Rufe Davis

The best Western Duo ever! Gene and Smiley.

A solo picture of the first great sidekick, Smiley Burnette.

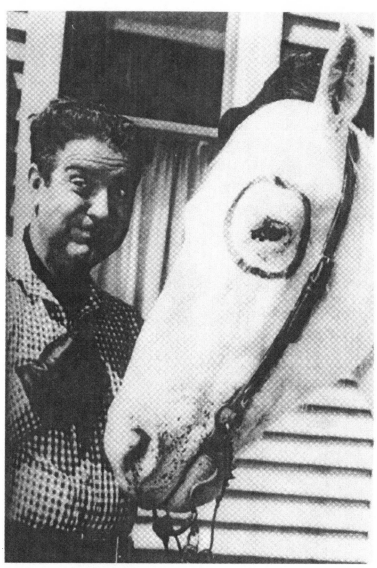

Smiley's horse would be called, at different times, Black-Eyed Nellie, Ring-Eyed Nellie, and finally simply Ring-Eye.

The best loved sidekick of all time, George "Gabby" Hayes.

George "Gabby" Hayes appeared with many western film icons.
Here he is with William Boyd, 1935

—with William Elliott, 1943,

—and Roy Rogers, 1945.

Eddie Dew is holding his six gun as Smiley looks on with Charles Miller in "Raiders of Sunset Pass" (1943). This was Dew's second, and last, starring film for Republic Pictures.

Smiley looks on as Sunset Carson shows how to give a fellow actor support

97

Smiley unhappily leers from behind the Durango Kid. Probably watching Gene do a scene with new sidekick, Pat Buttram.

Gene was obviously a better actor than he was given credit for if he could manage a smile for Sterling Holloway.

The first Autry-Burnette film under Republic Pictures banner. Note that Smiley's costume is not yet established.

"Waterfront Lady" (1935) Smiley appeared for Nat Levine at Mascot in this non-Autry vehicle.

*In "The Singing Cowboy" (1936) Smiley's name
appears before Champion's.*

In 1939 Smiley maintains a good strong billing.

The last film together at Republic Pictures (1942)
Smiley's name appears right under Gene's.

Smiley and Robert Livingston, here billed as Bob, did two episodes
of the John Paul Revere series together (1944). Note that it is billed
as a Smiley Burnette Production.

Smiley and Sunset Carson. Note Smiley's billing compared to the hero of the film, Sunset Carson. "Bordertown Trail" (August, 1944) was their second film together.

At least in the one sheets Smiley received top billing with Charles Starrett, something unheard of in most program B westerns. Notice he is billed as the "West's No.1 Comic" (1947).

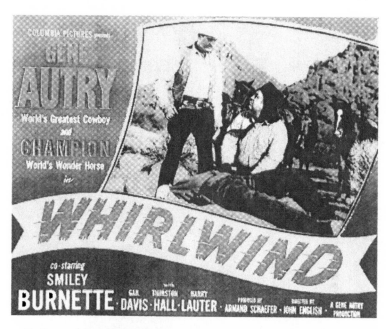

Smiley and Gene reteamed for this one film in 1951. Smiley is given good sidekick billing, but it's after Champion.

By the time Smiley reteamed with Gene Autry for his last six films (1953) his billing wasn't so good.

Top: Gene Autry and Pat Buttram in "Valley of Fire," from 1951.
Bottom: Buttram as Mr. Haney from the popular series, "Green Acres."

104

CHAPTER SEVEN
FUZZY WASN'T FUZZY, WAS HE?
—or—
WHAT'S IN A NAME?

As the saying goes, "What's in a name?" Well, if you were a movie studio in the '30s and '40s obviously plenty. Throughout this period, sidekick names like "Cannonball," "Whooper," "Chito," and "Fuzzy" were given to different actors through the whims of the studios who owned them. Some names like "Gabby" or "Smiley" became sacred cows, hands off, but other names were bandied about with reckless abandon.

The case of Fuzzy is simple to understand. An independent studio about to film a new western series produced by, of all people, comedian Stan Laurel and starring singing cowboy Fred Scott, loses its sidekick. The name in the script just happens to be "Fuzzy," same as the actor who was originally cast to play the part. When that actor walks away from the part, instead of giving the new sidekick a different name, the studio leaves the script the way it is, keeping the name "Fuzzy." They simply hire another well-known character actor to play the part. This simple act would have consequences later on.

In the case of other name changeovers it wasn't so simple.

Take the case of George Hayes. It's hard to imagine George as being called anything but "Gabby." But, from the summer of '35 through the summer of '39 people knew him as "Windy Halliday."

Windy rode, alongside Hopalong Cassidy, through twenty-two films before Republic Pictures offered Hayes a better contract. Cassidy producer Harry "Pop" Sherman was certainly reluctant to let him go, but he bid the sidekick farewell with one stipulation. Legally Hayes couldn't take the "Windy" moniker with him. Sherman had created the name for his Hopalong Cassidy series, and wasn't about to let George take it to Republic.

Sherman had given Hayes the kind of recognition that had eluded him through countless Westerns throughout the early '30s. As a matter of fact, Hayes wasn't originally signed to play Hoppy's sidekick. The producer knew that few filmgoers may know George Hayes by name, but his face was certainly recognizable from his numerous western film portrayals. Only in his forties at the time, Hayes specialized in playing old codger types. At first, Sherman signed Hayes to play different characters in the "Hoppy" series, but, when he caught on with the public, the role of Windy was created for him.

When George defected to Republic Pictures, the studio began to think of suitable replacement names. The nickname of Windy had been created because the character was a blowhard. Windy was constantly bragging about his feats of daring do, tangling with nasty outlaws, sometimes a dozen at a time, and getting away unscathed. Windy was full of hot air, a bit of a windbag. The name fit the character perfectly. Obviously Republic was looking for George Hayes to play the same type of character, but what name could they bestow upon their sidekick? "Gabby" Whitaker, so called for his gift of gab, was created and the name fit perfectly.

George Hayes would leave series work in '46, but he was so identified as "Gabby" Hayes that he was known by that name for the rest of his life. As a side-note, in larger budgeted films, he would be given a name other than Gabby. Ironically, in **Wyoming** (1947) with William Elliott, he is known as "Windy" (Gibson) and in **Untamed Breed** (1948), with Sonny Tufts, he is known as "Windy" (Lucas). Republic produced the former, while Columbia produced the latter film. Could these have been an in-joke aimed at his days working for Harry "Pop" Sherman?

George Hayes was so popular after his move to Republic Pictures that, Sherman would bill him as George "Gabby" Hayes in any Hopalong Cassidy films released or re-released in which he had co-starred prior to leaving the series.

The name of Whopper, although not well known today, was given to three different actors at RKO. Chill Wills was the first to use the name, when the studio cast him in a series starring western favorite George O' Brien. Wills would play the character in five films released from November of '38 through June of '39. He would then go on to a long lasting film career until his death in 1978.

In 1940, RKO signed Tim Holt for a series of Westerns and hired Emmett Lynn to play the character of Whopper. Obviously RKO liked this name. Lynn would be paired with singer Ray Whitley, who had also appeared with O' Brien, as a kind of sidekick duo to the popular Holt. Lynn would play Whopper in four films in the Holt series. In 1942, he would turn up at Republic Pictures for six films with Don Barry, five as his sidekick. He stayed at that studio for five episodes of the Red Ryder series, two with Bill Elliott and three with Allan Lane. During this time, he also ventured down to "Poverty Row" for three films alongside Eddie Dean at PRC. In '49, Lynn rounded out his sidekick days in the four Jim Bannon "Red Ryder" efforts for Eagle Lion Films. After he left RKO, and the Whopper character, Lynn never again had a steady character name to pin his career on. This would hurt many a sidekick. Without a steady character name, a sidekick would lack an identity for the audience to grow accustom to.

The last actor to play Whopper was Lee "Lasses" White. White would continue the role with Holt and Whitley through eight films. Two years later, in '44, White would turn up at Monogram Pictures as Jimmy Wakely's sidekick for twelve films. He would be known simply as Lasses. Lynn and White were so similar in appearance and actions that it is sometimes hard to tell them apart.

The character of Whopper was similar to the Windy/Gabby character in that he gained his name through the "whoppers" he would tell about his supposed heroic feats. Whopper was also an interesting anomaly in the realm of sidekicks in that the character, and not the actor, was the featured comic relief. RKO simply changed the actor, but not the name.

RKO would try this trick one more time. Richard Martin had played a character named "Chito" in the World War II picture *Bombardier* (1943) starring Pat O' Brien and Randolph Scott. The character proved popular, so RKO decided to move Chito back into the previous century for a western series based on the works of Zane Grey.

The character of Chito Jose Gonzales Bustamante Rafferty was a popular addition to the series. Martin rode with up and coming star Robert Mitchum in two pictures of the series. Mitchum then moved on to A films and was replaced by James Warren. After one picture with Warren, Martin asked for a twenty-five dollar raise and was greeted with his walking papers.

In their infinite wisdom, instead of giving Warren a sidekick with a different character name, RKO simply cast John Laurentz in the role of Chito Rafferty. But Richard Martin had created the Chito character, and, unlike the ever-changing Whopper character, audiences didn't accept Laurentz in the role. He played the role in two films, and then both he and Warren bid farewell to the series.

Like Gene Autry, Tim Holt had left a lucrative movie career to serve during World War II. He was an anomaly in the film business in that he could easily switch back and forth from A productions, like *The Magnificent Ambersons* and *The Treasure of the Sierra Madre*, to his B Westerns without batting an eye. With Holt back from the war, RKO embarked on one of their most enduring film series.

The post-war Tim Holt series holds up quite well today. He appears as a more assured, mature Holt than the actor who appeared on the screen before the war. The studio had also learned their lesson with the character of Chito Rafferty. They brought Richard Martin back, finally recognizing that it was the actor who made the role, not the other way around. The duo clicked at the box-office and they rode through twenty-six Westerns together. Holt was gracious with Martin, allowing him free reign with the series. Although considered the comical sidekick, Martin was taller and better looking than the hero. It was Chito who would very often woo the ladies, as well as being very adept in the action scenes. You could actually believe that this relationship could exist. The Holt series was one of the last to leave the theaters, bowing out with the film *Desert Passage* in May of '52.

Another misused sidekick name was "Cannonball."

When western film fans talk about Cannonball, they generally think of famous character actor Dub Taylor. But, for a time, another sidekick rode the range at Columbia Pictures using the name.

After a successful beginning in Frank Capra's film version of *You Can't Take it with You* (1938), Dub was cast in a B western series starring Bill Elliott as "Wild Bill Saunders."

After three of the "Saunders" pictures, the series became the "Wild Bill Hickok" series. Six of these were produced before it simply became the "Bill Elliott" series. After two in that series, Elliott once again became "Wild Bill Hickok" and was joined by Tex Ritter. Columbia appeared to be very fickle in what to name their hero. Elliott never really changed the way he played any of these characters, just the costume would change, so it really doesn't make any sense why the studio would continually play the name game in this way. Through it all, Dub was cast as Cannonball.

During this period, Dub also rode over to Republic Pictures where he did *One Man's Law* (1940) with Don "Red" Barry, but not as Cannonball. Barry, a man of small stature, didn't like sidekicks who were taller than him. In that aspect, Dub would have been perfect as a foil for him. One wonders why he didn't appear in more films with Barry, unless his Columbia contract precluded it, or Barry just didn't accept him as a regular.

Barry seemed to run through sidekicks like water through a bucket full of holes. Al "Fuzzy" St. John (6 films), Emmett Lynn (6 films – 5 as his sidekick) Wally Vernon (6 films), and Syd Saylor (1 film), all diminutive actors who played sidekick to Barry during his five years riding the range at Republic Pictures. Only "Arkansas" Slim Andrews, an extremely lanky, tall comic musician, towered above Barry in his two films with him, and he only played his sidekick in one of those, *The Cyclone Kid* (5/42). As Andrews remembers his time with Barry: *"He was extremely temperamental. He was a little guy who wouldn't do a scene with me unless he was sitting down or I was sitting down."*

Diminutive or not, Barry was a terrific celluloid cowpoke whose films hold up quite well. He was extremely versatile and would appear in his own B series while playing bad guys in other films, much like another small stature cowpoke, Bob Steele, would do. But Barry wanted more and left a successful western series to look for the brass ring. Unfortunately it never came. He would appear in the top ten favorite western stars from '42 through '45. Today, Barry is continually overlooked but, for my money, he is one of the best to appear in his own Republic series.

As for Dub, after appearing in the first film with the Elliott and Ritter team, *King of Dodge City* (8/41), he left the series. Columbia decided not to create a new sidekick, but to simply recast the Cannonball role. This is surprising due to the fact that Taylor had already established the role in thirteen films!

The choice of comedian Frank Mitchell, formerly of the stage and film comedy duo Mitchell and Durant, was extremely puzzling. Taylor was nicknamed Cannonball due to his roly-poly stature, but Mitchell was anything but round. There was no reason given for naming Mitchell "Cannonball." He played the role through the remaining seven entries in the Elliott/ Ritter series. Like RKO before them, Columbia saw nothing wrong with changing the actor, but keeping the character's name, even if it didn't fit.

The last with Mitchell as Cannonball, *Vengeance of the West*, was released in August of 1942. Realizing their mistake, Columbia had Dub Taylor back as Cannonball by October of the same year in a new series with Russell Hayden.

Dub was a tremendous musician, rivaling Smiley Burnette in his musical abilities. In *The Last Horseman* (6/44), his last film with Hayden, Dub is in his true element when he is given a segment in which he performs some of his musical act. His banter with Bob Wills and the Texas Playboys, as he plays "Camptown Racetrack" on the xylophone, shows what a talented and easy-going performer he could be. It isn't for all tastes, but you can't dispute his talent.

Taylor would do nine films with Hayden before joining Charles Starrett. After five films in the series, Starrett brought back a character he had played in an earlier film, the Durango Kid. The character renewed Starrett's popularity. Dub did seven in the Durango Kid series before Columbia unceremoniously replaced him with Smiley Burnette.

Starrett missed the rotund little comedian and was sorry to see him leave. *"I just loved working with Dub. He not only was a good comic, he was a good actor."*

Leaving Columbia in early '46, Taylor signed with Monogram Pictures to give support to singing cowboy Jimmy Wakely. Wakely had been a semi-regular in the Starrett series with Cannonball. It was a sad time for Taylor, leaving Columbia and winding up at Monogram.

Buck Taylor told me this about his father's move to Monogram. *"I don't think my dad was particularly happy ending up at Monogram and the Wakely series, but he did his best."* Wakely also went on record saying that he wasn't happy with Dub's slapstick humor, so the feelings between the two were probably tenuous at best. Wakely was not a big proponent of sidekicks, as can be testified by his comments elsewhere about Smiley Burnette.

Silver Trails (August, 1948), the seventh for Dub and Wakely, would introduce a dubious entry into the world of western heroes... Whip Wilson. Wilson was a cowpoke whose hat was almost as big as he was, plus a hairpiece that was unbelievably laughable.

Wilson would soon be given a series of his own. It seemed that Monogram was making a concerted effort to see how many western heroes they could have under contract who couldn't act.

It's sad to note that PRC, which was considered lower than Monogram, had Eddie Dean, a crooning cowboy who actually could do some acting. If Dean had been given the chance, he would have made a great western star at one of the bigger studios.

But Wakely, although an extremely talented musician, was way out of his league in the acting department. However, Whip Wilson would make Wakely look like Clark Gable. Whip Wilson, who welded a whip, was obviously given his own series by Monogram in an attempt to cash in on the popularity of Lash LaRue, another PRC product.

Columbia gave Taylor no trouble about taking the Cannonball persona with him. He would play Cannonball through fifteen films in the Wakely series, before discontinuing the character.

The upside to the story is that, Dub Taylor was one of the few sidekicks, Slim Pickens being another, who left his sidekick days behind to become a very respected and prolific actor. His last picture was *Maverick* with Mel Gibson and James Garner. He also became a favorite guest of Johnny Carson during his last years as host of the *Tonight Show*, and gained a whole new generation of fans with his Hubba Bubba Bubblegum and Pace Picante Sauce commercials.

As his star began to rise, Dub refused to talk about his days as Cannonball. But in his later years, through an outpouring of fan requests, he realized what a tremendous contribution he had made to the B Western and embraced his years as Cannonball. He is, and always will be, the Cannonball we all know and love.

Now we get to the case of Fuzzy, or should I say Fuzzys. Today, we remember Al "Fuzzy" St. John fondly for his days with Buster Crabbe and Lash LaRue, but it was another famous character actor who was instrumental in helping St. John acquire the nickname we remember him by.

John Forrest Knight was a popular character actor who had acquired the nickname of "Fuzzy" due to his raspy, or "fuzzy," voice. Leaving the name John Forrest behind Knight took the stage name Fuzzy Knight.

Like many western film sidekicks, Knight started on the vaudeville stage. Before long he was on Broadway. By 1933 he was appearing in films, starting with the Mae West classic *She Done Him Wrong*.

Like another character actor Roscoe Ates, who would also appear as a sidekick in Westerns, Fuzzy Knight would rely on an exaggerated stutter for laughs. This would eventually be played down when the Hays Office, the censors of the time, and local PTO groups, were afraid that kids might make fun of anyone who stuttered. Knight would still sneak the stutter in from time to time throughout his screen career. It wouldn't be as pronounced, but just the same it's there. It's amusing to see how inventive Knight would get with the stutter to confound his critics.

In 1936, Knight ventured into his first western series when he played Kermit Maynard's sidekick for two films at Ambassador Pictures. The same year he would move over to Grand National for one with Tex Ritter.

Knight was then signed to ride the musical range in a series of films for Spectrum Pictures. The series, produced by comedian Stan Laurel, was to star singer Fred Scott. Fuzzy Knight backed out at the last minute, and character actor Al St. John was signed to play sidekick to the crooner.

Spectrum never bothered to change the name of the sidekick in the script, and so St. John was called "Fuzzy" through all seven films with Scott. By the time all the films had been released, St. John was so identified with the nickname "Fuzzy" that he kept it as his own. From there St. John created the character of Fuzzy Q. Jones. With few exceptions, he would use this name throughout the rest of his career.

Al was a true screen veteran by the time he became a western sidekick, at one time even appearing as a Keystone Cop for Mack Sennett. Having popular comedian Roscoe "Fatty" Arbuckle as an uncle didn't hurt either. He worked with his uncle after leaving Sennett. By the early 1920s, St. John was appearing in his own comic shorts for companies such as Fox and Paramount.

By the late 1920s, St. John's career was on a downward slide and so he re-invented himself. He began appearing in Westerns supporting stars like Tom Mix, Bob Steele, John Wayne, Tom Tyler, Rex Bell, Johnny Mack

Brown, Tex Ritter, Buster Crabbe, Bob Custer, Bill Cody, and William Boyd before his Hoppy days. By the time he appeared in the Fred Scott series, St John had appeared in support of more western stars than George Hayes or any other sidekick.

After the Scott series ended, St. John appeared with Robert Livingston's brother, Jack Randall, in a couple of films, as well as films starring George Houston, Art Jarrett, and a Renfrew of the Mounties picture starring James Newill and Dave O' Brien.

St John was a very busy boy, but his real popularity was about to begin. In 1940, Producer's Releasing Corporation (PRC) put St. John under contract to appear as sidekick opposite Bob Steele in a highly fictionalized series based on the exploits of Billy the Kid. The films proved very popular, but Steele left PRC after six films in the series to join the Three Mesquiteers at Republic Pictures.

Inspired casting brought Flash Gordon/ Buck Rogers star Buster Crabbe to PRC where he took over the Billy the Kid role. The duo proved extremely popular and the action mixed well with the comedy. It was obvious that Crabbe and St. John had a genuine affection for each other, which came across on the screen much like Roy Rogers and Gabby Hayes. It's a shame that one of the bigger studios didn't pick them up.

Crabbe was a likeable hero and could really act! St. John began to perfect his Fuzzy character with this series, although from time to time he appears to slip into a Gabby characterization. This type of character flaw would happen often with St. John. It seemed like Al didn't know whether his character should be that of a younger or older type, and so he would slip in and out of both. One minute he would appear to be somewhat youthful, with a drop in the timbre of his voice; this would usually happen during his more serious moments. Then he would appear to be chewing his cud and seemingly appear as an older curmudgeon, similar to Gabby. An interesting side-note is that George Hayes was only eight years older than Al St. John. No matter what his shortcomings, Al "Fuzzy" St John is considered the third member of the sidekick hierarchy, along with George "Gabby" Hayes and Smiley Burnette.

After thirteen films in the series the Billy the Kid premise was dropped. Buster simply became Billy Carson, and Fuzzy played—well—Fuzzy.

Twenty-three films were released in the Carson series and then Crabbe abruptly left. As Crabbe tells it: *"We started my last movie at PRC on Monday and had it in the can on Thursday! That's when I decided I'd had enough and quit. They didn't even blink an eye. The next thing I knew they had replaced me with Lash LaRue."*

In all, from October 1941 through September 1946, Buster Crabbe and Al St. John made thirty-six films together. During the years that Fuzzy was churning out the Steele and Crabbe films, which on the average was one every two months, he was appearing in two other western series as well!

From November of 1940 through March of 1942, St. John appeared in six films with Don "Red" Barry at Republic Pictures. During this same period he was also appearing in the Lone Rider series for PRC, eleven with George Houston and six with Robert Livingston. Al "Fuzzy" St John has the distinction of being the only sidekick appearing in three western series at the same time!

From June of 1940 through September of 1946, St John played the sidekick in sixty-five films at two different studios! While Smiley and Gabby may have been considered the most popular sidekicks, Fuzzy St. John was definitely the busiest!

After Crabbe left PRC, Fuzzy St. John inherited the hero he is most associated with, Lash LaRue. LaRue had been appearing in the Eddie Dean series and proved to be as popular as the star. It's reported that Dean may have suggested LaRue be given his own series to get rid of him, but I'm sure that PRC came to that conclusion on their own. Especially when Buster Crabbe left an opening for a cowboy star.

In fairness to Dean, I believe that if he had been given a contract with Republic Pictures the singing cowboy would have given Roy and Gene a run for their money. Instead the very capable performer was stuck at PRC.

As for LaRue, his popularity is still a mystery to me. In "The Legends Live On," I compared him to a poor man's Humphrey Bogart, which is what hurt his career in the 40s. Since then I've noticed he brings someone else to mind. Watch one of his Westerns and listen closely to his voice. He's a dead ringer for Dean Martin!

Nevertheless, Lash and Fuzzy proved to be a popular two-some. Unfortunately they made only eight films at PRC before the series ended in '47. The very next year they signed a contract with Western Adventure Productions and made twelve more.

Their time together was brief and Fuzzy didn't take to Lash LaRue at first, believing he was responsible for the departure of Crabbe. As Lash tells it: *"Fuzzy and I worked together almost a year before he walked up to me one time and said, 'You know I wasn't going to like you, but you're all right,' From then on we became very close friends."*

The PRC films were released from February of '47 through December of the same year. If what Lash says is true, then they would have shot most of the PRC films before they made peace.

Al "Fuzzy" St. John appeared in his last film *Frontier Phantom* in February of '52. By that time he had appeared in more than ninety western films as the sidekick. Al "Fuzzy" St. John may have had his drawbacks, but he was always interesting to watch.

Now lets turn our attention to the original Fuzzy, Fuzzy Knight that is. It's hard to imagine two Gabbys or two Smileys appearing in films simultaneously, and both of them being successful. But, in the case of our two Fuzzys, they were both very successful in the sidekick arena.

Fuzzy Knight probably didn't appear in the Fred Scott films, for the independent Spectrum film company, because Universal Pictures offered him a contract to appear in a series with singing cowboy Bob Baker. Knight did four films with Baker, while appearing in one picture at Monogram with another singing cowboy, Jack Randall. It's interesting to note that Fuzzy Knight did his one film with Randall about the same time as Al St. John did his film with Randall.

Knight's most enduring partnership was with Johnny Mack Brown at Universal. Brown and Bob Baker would pair up for six with Knight, before Baker bid farewell to the series. Brown and Knight would do fifteen more before Tex Ritter joined them for a series of seven.

As if that weren't enough shuffling about, Universal tried a few more combinations. Knight would do one,

Arizona Trail, with Ritter in September of '43, and then *Frontier Law* with former Hoppy performer Russell Hayden in November of the same year. By early '44, Universal paired Ritter and Hayden, along with Knight, for two films *Marshal of Gunsmoke* (1/44) and *Oklahoma Raiders* (3/44).

New Universal western star Rod Cameron was then given able help by Knight in four films in 1944. During this series Knight tried to succeed where Smiley Burnette failed, by lending support to Eddie Dew in a western at Universal. *Trail to Gunsight* (8/44) even had the added attraction of Ray Whitley providing musical interludes, but Dew didn't catch on at Universal any better than he did at Republic. They wouldn't give up on him, however, and they paired Dew with Rod Cameron and Knight for two films the following year.

Next came a series of seven with Kirby Grant, who would go on to TV fame as *Sky King*. As Grant recalls:

"Fuzzy was a genuinely funny person. Some of the side-kicks were not really funny. They affected humor with their appearance and in little gimmicks they used, but Fuzzy had a great sense of what was funny. His comedy was not generally of the falling-into-the-horse trough type. A lot of what Fuzzy did for comedy was improvised right on the set. The lines, the bare bones, were there but Fuzzy fleshed them out with his own brand of humor and gimmicks, double takes, and things of that sort."

The next western series is a bit of a puzzle. Lippert Pictures signed former Hopalong Cassidy romantic side-kicks, Jimmy Ellison and Russell Hayden to a quickie series of six Westerns. The pairing of Ellison and his successor in the Hoppy series must have seemed like inspiration.

The six films were shot in a period of one month! Each film used the same cast. Knight was given co-star billing with Ellison, Hayden and another old-time sidekick, Raymond Hatton. The perplexing thing is that Knight and Hatton did not play recurring characters. They were reduced to supporting Ellison and Hayden; sometimes not even making an entrance until the movie was half over. With a running time of less than one hour, Knight and Hatton had limited screen time. The character choices were perplexing as well. For a western audience, who was used to seeing Knight as a humorous sidekick, it must have been jarring to see him end up as the villain as he occasionally did in these pictures.

Knight was back in form supporting Rex Allen in *Hills of Oklahoma* (5/50), appearing alongside fellow stutter comedian Roscoe Ates. This was a one-picture deal and his next prolonged stay was at Monogram in support of Whip Wilson.

Fuzzy Knight did a series of eight with Wilson. Andy Clyde, following his screen adventures with Hopalong Cassidy, had already appeared in twelve with the whip-welding hero.

Fuzzy Knight's last western series was a fairly good one. William Elliott, having left Republic, was now working at Allied Artists (formerly Monogram Pictures).

Elliott and John Wayne were the only two western stars at Republic Pictures during the '40s who were given A budget films to star in; Richard Dix had been their biggest star in the '30s. You could always tell whether Elliott's films were A or B pictures by the way he was billed. William Elliott was used for A films and "Wild Bill" Elliott for the B product. In the late '40s, Republic began to streamline their operation and Elliott was a casualty of the process.

Knight did four in the Allied Artists series, which were released from May of '52 through November of '53. Just before doing this series, Knight appeared in *Gold Raiders* in 1951. This film has the distinction of starring cowboy great George O' Brien and the Three Stooges!

Fuzzy Knight was very different from Al "Fuzzy" St. John in appearance and approach to comedy. Knight was a character actor who did and said things in a funny way; he wasn't above mugging when it was necessary. Knight had no particular costume attached to his character. Most of the time he played a different character in each film, from "Bullseye," to "Pinky," to "Echo," and "Banjo," even though the hero he was with might be the same from picture to picture. He could change his attitude and attire with each film depending on what the script called for. Because he had no distinctive character, he isn't as fondly remembered today as Gabby, Smiley, or Fuzzy St. John.

While Knight said and did things in an amusing way, Fuzzy St. John leaned heavily on saying and doing things in an outright broad and slapstick way. No subtlety, just out and out wide-eyed double takes and pratfalls. Like Andy Clyde, who had also appeared in Mack Sennett shorts, St. John was very adept at taking his time setting up a gag, whether it was comically mounting a horse or falling in a water trough. Like Smiley Brunette, he reveled in his buffoonery. St. John was lucky in that he was paired with two western heroes, Crabbe and LaRue, who didn't mind his taking the time to set up a funny gag. As far as Buster or Lash were concerned, St. John could get away with entering a serious scene, and pull off some sort of monkey business, and get away with it. It worked much better with St. John at PRC then it did at Republic. It might have been the overall cheesiness of the productions at PRC that made it work. Production values of a PRC film were already on the slender side and the antics of St. John just added to them. Smiley couldn't get away with it as well in the slick productions at Republic, although it would work in small doses.

No doubt, during the '30s and '40s, there were probably a few cases of mistaken identity when it came to the two Fuzzys. In 1953 there would be one more case of "Fuzzy Logic," and it would involve Buster Crabbe.

Crabbe was set to star in a new NBC television adventure show to be called *Captain Gallant of the Foreign Legion*. His producer, Harry Saltzman, who would go on to successfully co-produce the early James Bond movies, asked Crabbe who he would like as his sidekick in the new series. Naturally, Crabbe thought that Fuzzy St. John would be an excellent choice for his comic foil in the show, and asked Saltzman to look him up. It's at this point that the story gets...well...fuzzy. Fuzzy Knight was cast instead of St. John. How did it happen? Crabbe has given two different accounts of the event.

In an interview with author David Rothel, Buster recalls it this way: *"When we were looking for a fellow to play the sidekick role in the foreign legion series, I said to Harry Saltzman, the producer, 'when you get out to California, look up Al "Fuzzy" St. John.'*

"So when Saltzman got out to Hollywood, he called Fuzzy St. John in. Poor old Fuzzy went in loaded. That threw him out of the series. When I called Harry to check on things, I said, 'Well, Harry, did you find somebody?'

He said, 'Yeah, Fuzzy Knight.'"

Clearly in this interview, Crabbe makes it clear that St. John himself is to blame for his loss of the sidekick role due to a drinking problem. But, in another version, from the biography, "Buster Crabbe. A Self Portrait," by Karl Whitezel, Crabbe recalls the event differently.

"Saltzman asked who I'd like to have for the sidekick in the series. Since I'd always worked well with Al "Fuzzy" St. John, I suggested that, if the old Western association didn't get in the way, Fuzzy would be nice for a partner. We had worked together in over 37 films so I took it for granted the advertising executives, who were putting the television package together, knew about Fuzzy's identification with me. Soon I got a call from Saltzman telling me Fuzzy would be in New York the following day. I agreed to come to the office at that time so the contracts could be finalized.

*When I walked into Saltzman's large office, I saw instantly that a mistake had been made. The actor sitting in a chair talking to some men wasn't Al "Fuzzy" St. John. It was Fuzzy Knight, a venerable sidekick to many cowboy stars, but never to me. We had worked together in two films: **To the Last Man** in 1933 and **She Had to Choose** in 1934. I called Saltzman to one side. 'I didn't mean Fuzzy Knight. I was talking about Fuzzy St. John.'*

'I'm sorry, Buster, when you said "Fuzzy," we put out a call for a "Fuzzy" and he's what we came up with.'"

There you have it. Which story is the truth? One causes damage to St. John's reputation, while the other is simply an innocent mix-up. Either way things had come full circle. In 1937, Al St. John had replaced Fuzzy Knight in a series of Westerns and gained his nickname to boot. Now, in '53,

Fuzzy Knight replaced Fuzzy St. John in a part that was intended for him. It's a crazy world!

Today, Fuzzy Knight is probably better remembered for his role as Buster Crabbe's sidekick in the TV series or his stuttering schtick in countless supporting roles, like *Trail of the Lonesome Pine* or the 1951 version of *Showboat,* than a sidekick of any importance; even though he played that role with at least fifteen western stars over almost a twenty year period.

Like "Smiley" Burnette, the "Fuzzy" was used as his first name, not a nickname like Al "Fuzzy" St. John. Except for the nickname "Texas," in the Whip Wilson series, he never really had a continuing character name. Knight used the name "Fuzzy" sparingly, like the Roy Roger's picture, *The Cowboy and the Senorita* (1944) at Republic, which was also Dale Evans' first film with Roy. Smiley, at least, had the "Frog Millhouse" character at Republic, even though he later used his own name at Columbia Pictures. Identity was important to capture an audience.

Al St. John went the way of George "Gabby" Hayes and used the name "Fuzzy" as his character name in movies. With few exceptions, St. John used the nickname in his films, thus creating a distinct relationship with his fans. Even though he was stuck at a poverty row studio, as opposed to Knight who had the benefit of Universal Pictures and its top western stars, St. John had successful and steady relationships with two strong personalities, Buster Crabbe and Lash LaRue.

There was a distinct difference in the way Knight and St. John used the name Fuzzy. But this still didn't stop the confusion from happening, especially with both of them continually appearing so successfully in the same genre during the same period of time.

So when *was* Fuzzy not Fuzzy? That's easy! When he was the other Fuzzy. Now that's "Fuzzy" logic!

Fuzzy Knight was one of the most prolific sidekicks in the Western genre.

Al "Fuzzy" St. John, the third member of the sidekick hierarchy. Smiley Burnette and George "Gabby" Hayes are the other two.

Al working in the silents.

Al St. John in 1935, working with Guinn "Big Boy" Williams in "Law of the 45s." This is the first film based on William Colt Macdonald's Three Mesquiteers stories. Williams played Tucson (spelled Tuscon in the credits) and St. John played Stoney (again the spelling in the credits). The mesquiteers were a duo and not a trio in this film.

*Al made one film with Tex Ritter, "Sing, Cowboy Sing,"
released in 1937.*

*St. John is sharing a musical moment with Christine McIntyre
and Fred Scott in 1938. The Scott series is where St. John got the
nickname "Fuzzy."*

St. John and Don "Red" Barry in one of their films together at Republic Pictures. St. John would leave his Fuzzy character behind when at Republic.

St. John and Buster Crabbe were a perfect team. They made thirty-six films together.

Al and Lash LaRue. This was St. John's most famous pairing.
They did twenty films together.

A stellar cast appeared in "The Lonesome Trail" in 1943. From left to right are: Johnny Bond, Scotty Harrel, Jimmy Wakely, Fuzzy Knight, Jennifer Holt, Johnny Mack Brown, George Eldredge, Harry Strang, Tex Ritter, and (on the floor) Robert Mitchum.

Rod Cameron, Knight, and Ray Whitley from "Riders of Santa Fe," (1944).

Fuzzy Knight (center) and Kirby Grant (far right) in 1945.

The bottom of the barrel for Russell Hayden, Fuzzy Knight, Raymond Hatton, Jimmy Ellison, (with future Universal Pictures star Julie Adams). The quartet of western stars appeared in a series of six films all shot in one month.

Jim Bannon and Knight in the Whip Wilson feature,
"Stagecoach Driver," (1951).

Fuzzy Knight did much better for himself in 1952 and '53 with his last
western series, appearing with Bill Elliott in five films for Allied Artists.
The two are featured here with my favorite Lois Lane, Phyllis Coates,
in "Fargo," (1952). This was the second film in the series.

CHAPTER EIGHT
MAKING A LIST AND CHECKING IT TWICE
— OR —
THE END OF THE TRAIL FOR NOW!

I love B Westerns and the stars. They could shoot straight, play a guitar, and sing a song all while bouncing around on their favorite wonder horse, and we accepted it. But they were human.

With an acknowledgment to Tom Mix, and Ken Maynard, Gene Autry will always be the cowboy, singing or not, who set the stage for all who followed in the era following the advent of sound. Dick Foran, Jack Randall, Smith Ballew, Fred Scott, Bob Baker, Tex Ritter, Monte Hale, Jimmy Wakely, Eddie Dean, and Roy Rogers, all the way to Rex Allen all owe him a lot.

Len Slye – Leonard Sly on his birth certificate, the 'e' was added to "Sly" later, may have remained a member of the Sons of the Pioneers, or ended up at PRC as Dick Weston, if not for Gene leaving Republic Pictures, not once but twice, so that Roy Rogers had a chance to be born and shine as he did!

Although both he and Gene were the forerunners in the singing cowboy sub-genre the similarity ended there. They had their own characters and traveled in different worlds. Yates would revamp some of Gene's old story lines and give them to Roy, but the results would always be different. Even Smiley Burnette would react differently to Roy than Gene. I found him to be very agreeable in Roy's world and very enjoyable. Although Herbert J. Yates may have expected sparks to fly between Gene and Roy they never did. Their agendas were completely different. Roy held family in high esteem, while for Gene it was always business.

I once asked Peggy Stewart, who had worked with both stars, what the difference was between them. This is what Peggy said: *"With Roy, when the director yelled 'cut,' he would stick around and joke with us. He was just one of the guys. With Gene, when the director said 'cut,' his people would immediately surround him, while he was giving out orders for someone to buy this stock or sell that one. He was always business."*

Gene put Republic Pictures on the map and made the studio a viable contender. They became the leader in the B cowboy genre. Without Gene's contributions, and later Roy's, Republic Pictures may have simply been another Poverty Row studio, like PRC or Monogram.

Likewise, Smiley paved the way for sidekicks and Gabby refined it. They should both be remembered for their solid contributions to the B oater. All sidekicks to follow had these two to thank.

And what about the original pioneers in this industry? Before Gene, Roy, Tex, the Duke, Starrett, Hoppy or Johnny Mack Brown there was Broncho Billy Anderson, William S. Hart, Tom Mix, Buck Jones, Tim McCoy, Hoot Gibson, and Ken Maynard, not to mention Fred Thomson. Tom Tyler, Bob Steele, and George O' Brien should probably be added as well. Although they were not innovators in the western genre, their contributions to silent and sound Westerns shouldn't be ignored.

It doesn't really matter that Mix falsified his bio to make him appear more adventurous. He set the pace for the fancy dressed heroes who rode the range of Republic Pictures. He and Hart were the first to introduce the trusty steed, Tony and Fritz respectively. They set the pace for Champion, Trigger, and Topper, all the way to Koko.

Add Leo Maloney to the list as well. He should be given his due for the pioneering efforts he made in the western genre. And how about Harry Carey, who was in a class by himself? The early films he did with a young director by the name of Jack Ford, who would later be known as John Ford, where classic examples of the every man later exemplified by Gary Cooper, Randolph Scott, Joel McCrea, and James Stewart.

William Boyd was a big star in silent films, and it looked like there was great promise for him when "talkies" took center stage. Sadly, he lost his career due to a case of mistaken identity. But we wouldn't have had the Hopalong Cassidy that we remember fondly if it wasn't for this. Out of tragedy came something terrific. It also helped to straighten out the wild life of the star; he actually took on the clean living traits of the character he played on film.

Let's not forget Tom Keene, Lane Chandler, Bob Custer, Rex Bell, Kermit Maynard, Wally Wales, Al and Jack Hoxie, Reb Russell, Buffalo Bill, Jr. and Buddy Roosevelt, all the way to Art Mix. They kept the western film a blazin' until it found solid ground in the mid-thirties.

A good ol' B Western is a safe bet for the family. We know that "Wild Bill" Elliott, Don "Red" Barry, Allan "Rocky" Lane, Tim Holt, "Sunset" Carson, any combination of the Three Mesquiteers, and Charlie Starrett, are the heroes and that Roy Barcroft, Kenne Duncan, Charles King, LeRoy Mason, I. Stanford Jolley or George Chesebro will probably be the villians.

There's something healthy about the renewed interest in these stars. It's a longing to get back to the basics of what they represented. The sad thing is that most of them are gone. Roy and Gene died within a few months of each other. Dale Evans followed a few years after her husband, and Rex Allen was taken from us long before his time. At this writing Monte Hale and Herb Jeffries are still with us, as are a few of those who were in support of the heroes.

At the Western film festivals, we have taken to honoring the stars of western films and TV shows of the '50s and '60s. They're fun to talk to, but how I long to once again be in the company of Lash LaRue, Rex Allen, and Dale Evans. It was a thrill to see Gene Autry talk to a crowd in Scottsdale, Arizona and, even though he was very frail, he held the audience in the palm of his hand for the better part of an hour.

I enjoy talking with Patrick Curtis, whose father was a director at Republic Pictures, and was a child actor there. Cheryl Rogers-Barnett and her husband, Larry, always give me interesting accounts of the times at Republic Pictures and, of course, great anecdotes about Roy and Dale. And my friend Buck

Taylor never ceases to amaze me with stories about his father, Dub. He is a true gentleman.

I think about the times I've spent watching these icons on the silver screen and how I've talked with many of them. The ones that I loved the most, John Wayne, Roy Rogers, and Clayton Moore are gone, and I will never be able to meet them, at least not in this life, but I was able to talk with George Montgomery, Ben Johnson, Harry Carey, Jr., Denver Pyle, Mary Ellen Kay, and Peggy Stewart who were there and rode the trails with these stars. These are moments that I treasure.

The B Westerns, and their stars, had jumped off the silver screen and onto the smaller TV screen by the time I was old enough to discover them. I feel fortunate that I found them, and that I've been able to meet some of the stars. I thank each one of them. I never want to tarnish any of the heroes, but I don't want to simply write drivel that states well-worn facts about their careers either. I write about the things I would like to read about; their lives, careers and relationships, warts and all. That's what interests me and I hope you as well.

Larry Barnett, Roy and Dale's son-in law, told me a story about Roy Rogers that best sums up what I've been trying to say.

"Roy was very frail during the last few weeks of his life. He would sit back on the sofa, in front of the TV, and watch some of his old Republic movies. That's about all he had strength to do. He had me sit there with him. He would just lie back on the sofa and watch these old movies. One time we were watch-

ing some old footage of a Republic Pictures employee picnic. It showed the employees and their families having a good time when suddenly Herbert J. Yates entered the scene. He started playing with the kids and talking and laughing with the employees. Roy sat straight up and then he leaned over, just staring at Yates on the TV set. Then, under his breath, more to himself then to me, he said, 'Well what do ya know. I have proof that the son of a gun was actually human.'"

They all were. The stars, the producers and directors, all of them were human. But for just an hour or so they could make us feel good about life. Good would beat out evil every time. And, even though some of them had their own personal demons to fight, they were invincible on the silver screen. They were our best friends and we still love to spend time with them. The hope of meeting them personally is gone, but we feel like we've known them all along. We feel like we've ridden the Hollywood trail right along with them.

EPILOGUE

This has been a difficult book to write. Many times I've gone through the different chapters and changed things that I may not agree with anymore, or that I've found discrepancy with.

I really had a difficult time working on the chapter about Smiley Burnette and his career. Many times I would go back to that chapter and revise or omit certain things that I had said. After reading and re-reading the chapter, and viewing and re-viewing his films, I came to appreciate Smiley much more then I had to begin with. Many things I had originally said I no longer felt. I could see certain nuances to his character that I hadn't noticed before. Originally, I felt that he wasn't capable of supporting the A players in a larger budgeted film, but I now feel that I was wrong. He was so good at what he did that it was hard to give him credit. He made it look so easy!

Watch him work with Gene, and then watch him work with Roy, and you'll see him adjust his character to fit the cowboy. Of course Gene and Roy treated him differently on screen as well, which means that he really was reacting to the hero. That's called acting!

I still feel that, given too much to do, he could wear out his welcome, as in the films with Eddie Dew, Sunset Carson, and to a certain extent Charles Starrett.

It's a shame that Republic made it look like they were building Smiley up into a powerhouse star, with co-star billing with Roy, his own "Smiley Burnette Productions" and his name above Sunset Carson's. All the while Gabby Hayes was actually being built up to possibly replace him through strudy roles in A and B pictures and endearing himself to the public. Gabby remains the most endearing sidekick, but I've gained a new appreciation for Smiley.

I also must admit to gaining new admiration for Gene Autry. I was never really a fan of his, until I started researching this book, and now I must admit that he has won me over. I'm still not quite sure what the secret to his popularity is, but I look forward to watching his films, especially the ones he made for Columbia Pictures. These films show a very self-assured Gene Autry and the films are slick entertainment.

You need to know that, by writing this book, I have gained a great appreciation for these stars. This has been a great experience for me, and I hope that by reading these stories you've gained something as well.

I started out on this odyssey with hopes of simply sharing my knowledge and research with you. What I came away with is more of an understanding of what these people mean to you and me. And that's a lot!

—Charlie LeSueur
June 2003

Some of Republic Pictures stable of stars circa 1945. From left to right: Sunset Carson, Robert Livingston, Allan Lane, Dale Evans, Roy Rogers, Bill Elliott, and Don Barry. This publicity photo was for Roy and Dale's feature, "Bells of Rosarita." The other stars joined in to round up the bad guys for the finale of the film.

Gene Autry, in 1974, sitting behind his desk and running a dynasty.

*Two of the
Singing Cowboys
from the 1940s:*

Eddie Dean, circa 1980

and Monte Hale, 1985

Stars, Buster Crabbe, Richard Arlen, Fuzzy Knight, and Dan Duryea with the man who started it all, Broncho Billy Anderson (sitting). This 1965 publicity photo taken for Alex Gordon's "The Bounty Killer."

Western Legends, from left to right: Ken Maynard, Rex Lease. Tom Keene (behind Lease), Bob Steele, Hoot Gibson, Raymond Hatton, and Guinn "Big Boy" Williams.

146

Charles Starrett in 1982.

Smiley Burnette with Elvis Presley, during Burnette's time on "Petticoat Junction."

Charlie leading one of his question and answer sessions. Seated from left to right are: Western author Matt Braun, George Montgomery, Peter Breck, Director Burt Kennedy, Buck Taylor, and Mary Ellen Kay.

Charlie pictured with Herb Jeffries, "The Bronze Buckaroo."

Beauties and the Beast. Left to right; Mary Ellen Kay, Charlie, Ruth Terry, and Peggy Stewart at the National Festival of the West, held in Scottsdale, Arizona.

About the Author:

Charlie LeSueur is a film historian, writer, and musician. Besides being the author of *Riding the Hollywood Trail* and *The Legends Live On,* Charlie has enjoyed musical success through 2002 - 2003 with two of his own country songs "Who's Your Daddy?" and "Move It Little," Both songs made it onto the independent country charts top twenty. He also made it to the European top 50 performers list.

Charlie continues to conduct the question and answer sessions at the **National Festival of the West**, held in Scottsdale, Arizona, which he has been doing since 1991, as well as performing and lecturing throughout the country.

Other Books By CHARLIE LeSUEUR:
The Legends Live on: Interviews with the Cowboy Stars of the Silver Screen

Charlie LeSueur has been entertaining audiences with his music and acting since the age of fourteen. An Arizona native, he now lives in Gilbert, Arizona, with his wife, Dawn. After appearing in over 500 commercials and many local television shows such as: *Chrome Highway, Arizona Sportsman,* and *Hoover's Place,* Charlie decided to take his love and knowledge for vintage western movies and put it to good use.

The Legends Live On: Interviews with the Cowboy Stars of the Silver Screen is the result. Charlie has also been involved with The National Festival of the West, which is held at Scottsdale, Arizona. It was at the festival where many of the interviews in this book took place.

Printed in the United States
201890BV00002B/283-327/P

9 781589 851047